"I first met Ruth when she was sixteen ye[...]o tell my listeners and me about the mornin[...]a a sighted person in the driver's seat, of cou[...]1 her mom if she could come in and cohost t[...]r her, and we've kept in touch ever since.

I thought I was aware of most of her life and career highlights as the years unfolded, but I wasn't; not until I read this book. When did she find time to get a Master's degree, visit more than twenty countries, teach a course at the University of Toronto, and so much more?

This book feels like you are walking beside Ruth as she experiences every small, medium and large life-impacting event. It reads like a motivational novel, and it's a page-turner.

If you are looking to be inspired, this book is for you. If you are just looking for a good read, you've found it."

–Bill Robinson, radio broadcaster and journalist

"*Love Is Blind* is an absolute delight of a book. Ruth Vallis' recollections of growing up blind are filled with fascinating details—from her poignant tales of navigating boarding school at age six to crossing Ontario on a tandem bike to fight for hospital programs. It's a remarkable picture of a remarkable life."

–Clive Thompson, author of *Coders: The Making of a New Tribe and the Remaking of the World* and contributing writer, *New York Times Magazine*

"From the first page Ruth's precise sharp wit and shining singular vocabulary draw the reader effortlessly into an adventure of the human spirit. With echoes of campfires and stories recited between elders. The pure winds of generations quietly walking the well-trodden forests of time.

This book is written with a humbling and generous voice that echoes within the rhythms of our own lives. Never once whilst reading this book will you ever consider Ruth to be blind. The pure voice of the human spirit expressing simple truths that we usually take for granted. Ruth's journey shines a light on the path that love carves out for those with the raw courage to give without expectation and to love unconditionally.

A wonderful first book."

–Claire Jennings, film and television producer

"[Ruth Vallis] astutely describes the hurdles posed by blindness and the inspiring manner in which she overcame them... A thoughtful, edifying, and moving remembrance."

–*Kirkus Reviews*

LOVE
IS BLIND

RUTH E. VALLIS

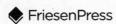 FriesenPress

Suite 300 - 990 Fort St
Victoria, BC, V8V 3K2
Canada

www.friesenpress.com

ISBN
978-1-5255-9362-8 (Hardcover)
978-1-5255-9361-1 (Paperback)
978-1-5255-9363-5(eBook)

1. *Biography & Autobiography, People with Disabilities*

Distributed to the trade by The Ingram Book Company

CONTENTS

PREFACE

Hello, my name is Ruth Vallis.

This is the way I always started my presentations when speaking at medical conferences. I wanted those in attendance to be certain they were listening to the person listed in the program.

Besides the usual sponsor logo–laden swag, attendees would receive a prospectus outlining the education and professional achievements of each presenter. My bio wasn't notably any different from anyone else's, but that's because it didn't include anything personal. Once introduced, I would proceed to the podium, my lecture notes in one hand and a guide dog harness grasped in the other. Then would come the shuffling of feet and a wave of murmurs that was followed by the rustle of flipping pages as people re-read my biography, looking to see where they had missed the word "blind." It wasn't there. After all, I was there as a physiotherapist and hydrotherapist, sharing expert knowledge in pain management, arthritis, etc. I would never claim to be an expert in blindness—I am simply a person who happens to be blind. Invariably, after the presentation, people would surround me with all sorts of questions, many of them not related to my topic but, instead, personal ones. Frequently, their parting comment would be that I should write a book about my life and what led to my success. However, I cannot do that without talking about Peach. She's my mother. I nicknamed her Peach when I was a teenager. I love peaches, and the truth is that she was a real peach—soft and sweet on the outside and with a hard nut in the middle!

William Ross Wallace penned, "the hand that rocks the cradle / Is the hand that rules the world." Indeed, Peach rocked me and, at the same time, she was my ruler and my world. As the decision was made that I would have to board at a school for the blind from the age of six, Peach reluctantly sent me away saying, "Ruthy, I do not know what will become of you, but you must go away to school to learn to read Braille. I can't teach you Braille, but you must learn to read; for, if nothing else, you must be able to entertain yourself!"

Now, dear reader, is the time to make a cup of tea or pour a glass of wine and come along on a journey that will take you from my birth to Peach's death. In between, you will learn about me being the youngest of the first group of blind children integrated into the public school system in Canada. Later, you'll read about Peach encouraging me to go off to England to study and the enormous challenges of being a blind person discovering London alone. Then, we will return home to find a job and start a career.

Through it all, there is Peach and many others—some who will block my path and others who will facilitate my journey. By the end, I hope that you will see how any child, with love, encouragement, and firm direction, can become independent and successful. Furthermore, you will believe in the strength of women and how, through working together for good, we can change the world!

CHAPTER 1

March 16, 1960, was shrouded in one of the worst blizzards of the winter. My father was at work, so when Peach went into labour, she had to call a taxi. As she entered the cab, she asked the driver if he had ever delivered a baby. He said that he had not. She suggested today might be the day, at which point he took off so quickly that she barely had time to close the door before he was helping her out and into the hospital. A few hours later, she was finally holding me in her arms, the little girl she had always hoped for and was determined to name Ruth.

I am sure that the first thing she did was rock me and sing me a lullaby. She was constantly singing or whistling, especially when sitting in one of her favourite rocking chairs. Peach was admired throughout the neighborhood as the woman who could rock three babies at once. She would rest infant Paul against her abdomen while balancing toddlers John and Christopher on opposing knees. I am not certain what she sang to the boys, but my lullaby was the Advent hymn, "Thou Didst Leave Thy Throne." She always managed to get the verses mixed up, but never the chorus: "O, come to my heart, Lord Jesus, there is room in my heart for thee." That large, strong, and confident woman, along with that chorus, became my comfort. I was ten years old before my brothers' constant teasing made me reluctantly decide it was time to stop sitting on her rocking lap.

Peach was a townie. A big city girl from St. John's, Newfoundland. She was an imposing figure with a very erect posture of five feet eight inches tall. Her skeletal frame was large and well-padded to about two hundred pounds. Her big, soft hands never held the hand of a child but, rather, enveloped them with a strength that said, *you need never fear*. She did everything very quickly, but nothing was as quick as her wit. She left Newfoundland in 1950, following two older sisters, simply for the adventure. She quickly adjusted to life in Toronto after getting an office job with Woolworths and joining St. Mary the Virgin Anglican Church.

My father came from round the bay—Fortune Bay, in fact. He left his tiny community, only accessible by sea, to join The Royal Regiment of Canada in Nova Scotia. He spent the next thirty-three months marching through the war zone of Europe. He was far too gentle a soul for soldiering. The battles left him with a hearing deficit and what we would now refer to as post-traumatic stress disorder, or PTSD. He was quiet and agreeable. His humour was corny, and he was always ready to assist with any request.

Dad didn't return to Newfoundland after the war. Initially, he went back to Nova Scotia for an education and then on to Toronto to find a job and some peace of mind. Suitable work was not easy to come by, but he did find friendship and more at St. Mary the Virgin Anglican Church.

Although post-war mental illness carried an enormous stigma and was mostly not talked about, he admitted to Peach that he occasionally felt depressed. With her usual optimism, she assured him that he would never be depressed again and that together, they could conquer anything. She explained that they would not be just a married couple, but an unconquerable team. The poor guy didn't know what hit him.

After just one year of marriage, John was born: a quiet, gentle boy who enjoyed reading, writing poetry, and soaking up the beauty of nature. Christopher came along twenty months later. As is typical of families, right back to biblical times, the second child could not have been more different than the first. Christopher was strong and athletic with a passively defiant spirit. There was no doubt that both boys had a little of each parent in him, but John was his father's son and Christopher, his mother's.

Paul came along thirteen months after Christopher and, again, could not have been less like his predecessor. While Christopher had a mass of curly dark hair, Paul had fair skin, fair hair, and blue eyes. He was colicky by night and listless by day. It is hard to imagine that the man Peach later described as her handsome, prosperous-looking son was the same one she had described in infancy as resembling a tennis ball in a bonnet. Although every mother says that she does not have a favourite, among the boys she had a little extra affection for Paul. Perhaps it was his frailty in his first few months of life or his sharp wit, which she always feared would get him in trouble. Whatever the reason, she adored him.

I came next, and Ralph was born eighteen months after me. Because of our close ages, we were great buddies. He was a combination of sensitivity and toughness. He was just as happy playing football with his friends or catch with Dad as he was making Peach a cup of tea or putting rollers in her hair.

If Peach loved John for his gentleness, Christopher for his strength, and Paul for his capabilities, she loved Ralph because he was the youngest, which gave him some sort of special designation. That child doesn't have to do or be anything; they just *are*.

The doctor suggested that perhaps five children was enough—at least, that was Dad's story. However, Peach said she stopped at five because each successive child had a narrower face than the one before, with eyes getting closer together, and she was worried that if she kept going, she would eventually give birth to a Cyclops.

We lived in a modest semi-detached house in the West End of Toronto. Dad worked for the Mason & Risch piano company, but the work was not steady. When there were pianos on order, he went to the factory, but when there was no work, he stayed home. Peach dreaded the stay-home times, as it put a terrible financial strain on the household, but she understood that Dad's undiagnosed and untreated PTSD meant that the likelihood of holding down full-time employment was not high. At the piano factory, he would occasionally have unexplained outbursts, during which he would overthrow his work bench and then, just as suddenly, calmly pick everything up and carry on. Only a very tolerant employer would put up with that, and they did.

One might ask why Dad didn't go to the Department of Veteran's Affairs (DVA) and inquire about a disability pension. Peach asked that question a few times, and Dad's answer was always that he went to fight for the country and not to be supported by the government. The DVA would occasionally send letters asking if they could do anything to help, but the letters were always discarded.

Peach was a very strong, bright, and capable woman. She could have easily worked full-time, and that would have made a great difference to us, but she would not. She knew that it would have helped us financially, but it would have harmed Dad psychologically. She was very sensitive to the wounded soldier's ego, and she believed that if she went out and did what he could not by bringing home amounts of money that he could not make, it would be more hurtful than helpful. She felt that it was better for all of us to suffer a little than for him to suffer a lot. To understand that, one only has to understand love and remember that she had promised him that he would never be depressed again.

Once Ralph was in school all day, Peach did go to work, but it was only a part-time job. The phrase "we can't afford it" was a common refrain, and yet, my parents didn't argue about money. When I asked about it years later, they quipped that you can't argue about something you don't have. Then they explained that they believed that when money, or the lack thereof, is allowed to come in the door, love goes out the window. They assured me that one should never worry about money because God is faithful and will always provide, and He did. We were not unhappy. We were very involved in church activities, had picnics in High Park, and had lots of fun with the other children of the neighbourhood. However, there are many things that influence the choices we make in life, and my parents' sacrifices did not go unnoticed by me.

Peach would have liked a clothes dryer. Seven people wear a lot of clothes and use a lot of sheets and towels, but we couldn't afford one. She did laundry twice per week and had to hang everything in the basement in the winter and on lines in the backyard in the better weather. Dishes were washed by hand and, if we went anywhere, we walked or took public transit.

Dad came home most Fridays with a pay envelope that contained his cash wages. He would hand it over to Peach and, together, they would allocate money for the church, groceries, other bills, and bus tickets for Dad to get to work. If there was anything left, it would go into the bank. One week, Dad asked Peach for thirteen dollars, which was over a third of his pay. She inquired why he needed so much money. He explained that he owed it to the man on the coffee truck at work. I quietly sat by and took in the whole conversation as I did on many occasions. Dad said that he liked a coffee with the other fellows, and he sometimes had a cream doughnut with it. Peach was horrified at the extravagance, but she gave him the money. Even at a very young age, my heart grieved to think that a working man, and even more, a wounded soldier, had to almost beg for money to buy a coffee and doughnut. It was then that I promised myself that I would get an education and, one day, get a good job so I could buy Peach all the things she wanted and buy Dad all the cream doughnuts his heart desired or stomach could hold. In fact, I told Peach that I was going to be a doctor when I grew up. I loved the smell of a hospital and could not imagine a more wonderful job than working in one.

Perhaps one of the main keys to the success of their overall relationship was that they both ascribed to the philosophy that one should not sweat the small stuff. Of course, the success of that thinking will depend upon how one defines small. As their motivation and thoughts on everything was driven by their faith and trust in God, almost everything was small.

Before my third birthday, however, the definition of small stuff would be stretched to the limit.

CHAPTER 2

In the days before ultrasound, people would often ask an expectant woman whether she was hoping for a boy or a girl. Most would reply that it didn't matter as long as the baby was healthy. Of course, everyone expects the child to be healthy, seldom giving much thought to any other possibility, and rarely is anyone prepared when the baby is not perfect.

Life for our family was normal for my first two-and-a-half years. However, there was a day, the date not specifically noted, that changed everything.

I dropped a penny on the floor and didn't immediately pick it up. Instead, I felt around the rug for it. My father pointed at it, but I did not acknowledge or follow his gesture. He called for Peach, and she also observed the unusual behaviour. Not certain what to think, Peach took me to the doctor, who gave her the shocking news that I had suddenly and inexplicably gone blind.

Peach had a sister, Helen, who'd had limited vision as far back as anyone could remember. She'd also had painful contracted knees in childhood, which my grandparents had massaged straight. By the age of forty-nine, she was functionally independent but totally blind. Nevertheless, my parents had no reason to suspect that any of their children would suffer the same fate. My mother's deep faith in God, however, gave her the strength to deal with this.

The cause of my loss of sight remained a mystery for the next three years. I, like my Aunt Helen, developed painful swollen knees and suffered a series of falls because they would suddenly give out. I tore every pair of tights and trousers I owned, which was more upsetting than the pain. On one occasion, my paternal grandmother, Nanny Vallis, was visiting from Newfoundland. I was given a new soft cotton outfit that included a pair of trousers with a ruffle around the ankles and a top with the same ruffles around the neck and cuffs. I was so excited to have new clothes (as I often had hand-me-downs from a girl up the street) that I begged Peach and Nanny to let me put it on and show it to the neighbours. As soon as I stepped outside, I fell and tore a big hole in one knee. I was devastated, thinking my beautiful new outfit was gone forever, but Peach was unfazed.

Peach could knit anything, but she never enjoyed sewing. Be that as it may, mothers often don't do what they want to do, but what they must do. She secretly huddled with Nanny and, together, they removed the ruffle from the bottom of each leg, cut the legs to the length of Bermuda shorts, and sewed the ruffle back on. When they brought them to me, I was over-whelmed with renewed joy. My outfit was back and even more wonder-ful, as it was summer and the shorts were cooler. The ruffles covered each bruised and battered knee. The transformation of those clothes may have been the first time I heard Peach say, triumphantly, "There is more than one way to skin a cat."

During that visit from Nanny, I made a relationship faux pas from which I would not easily recover. I, the only girl, was supposed to be seated at the dinner table beside my grandmother, which was thought by many, especially her, to be a prized place of position. Well, according to family lore, I did not eat my dinner, but simply sat quietly crying. Nanny inquired as to what was the matter, but I would not say. Peach then asked me what was wrong. My reply was that I wanted to sit beside my mommy. Nanny was horrified. Peach, on the other hand, was secretly delighted—we adored each other, and she was pleased to think that her mother-in-law could not pull any affection rank—not where I was concerned, anyway.

God only knows what she recounted to the other relatives at home in Newfoundland, but a few weeks later, my parents received a letter from her. Nanny wrote these oft-repeated words: "Poor, dear, sweet Ruth, living in a world of her own. You should put her in a home where people can look after children like her."

Peach asked Dad, "Who is she talking about, Lester?"

Dad, never wanting confrontation, just said softly, "I don't know, Blanche."

"No, and I don't either," said Peach. Referring to Nanny, Peach punctuated the end of the conversation with, "Damn fool!"

Before there was an opportunity to investigate why I was blind or falling, I developed tonsillitis. It was recommended that my tonsils be removed. My mother agreed, but my father said no. He was not comfortable with excising bits of the body God gave us. Unfortunately, I became increasingly ill, and my father's hand was forced. I recall well the last few days of my stay in hospital, but I have no recollection of the period following the surgery. Only many years later, when I overheard Peach telling someone of the incident, was I compelled to ask questions.

In twenty-first-century medicine, it is standard procedure to get consent for any surgery, which includes an explanation of the process and possible complications. In 1964, this was almost unheard of, and trust in the medical profession was absolute. After all, a tonsillectomy is a common procedure, so what was there to fear?

Well, in my case, it appeared there was plenty. I was not recovering from the surgery. I became increasingly weak and pale. The doctor could not explain my failure to thrive. He asked my parents to take me home, as he felt being in my own environment with my brothers around might help me improve. Not owning a car, my father hired a taxi, and as soon as they carried me into the cab, I started to vomit blood. Apparently, the number one complication of a tonsillectomy is haemorrhaging, and I had been haemorrhaging but swallowing the blood, leaving the doctors and nurses unaware. Peach described a horrific scene of hospital staff rushing me back inside. Fear gripped my parents as I was taken away, my skin a colour of grey that defied description, my eyes rolled back in my head and my body completely limp. My parents and the taxi were covered in blood. With great sadness, Peach recalled her desperate feeling of helplessness.

After waiting anxiously for news, the doctor came out and explained to Peach and Dad that they were doing what they could. I was haemorrhaging badly, and my parents needed to be prepared for the worst. Needless to say, no parent is ever prepared for that. My father was feeling guilty, worrying that he had held the surgery off for too long. Peach was feeling guilty, worrying that she should have listened to my father and not permitted the surgery at all. Peach said that she could not bear the thought of losing me, and so began the bargaining with God. He could have anything except her little Ruthy. Time stood suffocatingly still, but eventually, the doctor called my parents into a room where I was strapped to a board with blood trans-fusing into my body. Taking my other hand, Peach said "Hello Ruthy," and I replied, "Mommy?" Years later, with emotion still fresh after decades, she recalled it was the sweetest word she had ever heard.

My recollection of the whole thing started some time later. I had always loved listening to and trying to make music. A shop in our neighbour-hood had a little horn instrument for sale at the extravagant price of four dollars. I wanted it desperately, but Peach repeatedly said no. Nevertheless, I was delighted when Peach arrived at the hospital with that horn. I was in a room with five other children, and there was so much noise that my trying to get a tune out of my instrument was likely no extra insult to the ears. I had also heard somewhere that blind people wear dark glasses, so I agitated for a pair until Peach said that I could wear her sunglasses while in hospital. What could make a budding blind musician feel better than a pair of dark glasses and a horn?

Peach visited regularly, and I got stronger. It was on one of those visits that a nurse marvelled at how Peach could look after a household, care for four children at home—Ralph not yet three years old—and come to visit me. Things would have been a lot better for me if she had just smiled politely and said nothing. However, she innocently commented that things were even more complicated because one of my brothers, Paul, had chicken pox. With that, I was whisked away into quarantine.

Remember, this was 1964, so quarantine for a child meant a bare room with a metal-sided crib and no radio, television, toys, or visitors. For a blind child, it was solitary confinement. There was only the nurse who brought me metallic-tasting orange juice straight from a can and Arrowroot biscuits while administering my eye drops. I can still taste the juice and cookies. I asked if I could have my horn and sunglasses. I was informed that all my things had to be cleaned. I never saw my horn, or anything else, again. At the tender age of almost five, I discovered that when anything with plastic is placed into an autoclave, apparently with a steam temperature above the boiling point, nothing survives. Yes, it killed the possibility of chicken pox germs—as well as any hope I might have ever had of being the next Louis Armstrong or Miles Davis.

One of the most important things we can do for children is give them a sense of safety and security. I always had that with my Peach. While in quarantine, I asked a nurse why Peach wasn't visiting me. I was told that she was very busy at home with my brothers and laundry. I assured the nurse that laundry would never keep Peach from me. The nurse was surprised at my confidence in our relationship, and when she relayed my comments to my mother, Peach stated emphatically that I was correct and was reassured that I understood that she would always do everything in her power to be there for me when I needed her.

Some months later, I was taken to Dr. James Boon, a noted paediatric rheumatologist at the Toronto Hospital for Sick Children. He scheduled me for a biopsy of my knees to try and determine why I was suffering with the hot, red, swollen, and unstable joints.

The night before the procedure, he came to see me. Immediately, he noticed that my eyes were also inflamed. The biopsy was called off as he realized the connection. I was diagnosed with Still's disease, an aggressive form of juvenile rheumatoid arthritis that attacks joints and can also cause acute inflammation of the eyes or around the heart. Dr. Boon determined that this is what had caused me to go blind and referred me to the hospital's head of ophthalmology, Dr. Jack S. Crawford, for examination and possible treatment. Dr. Crawford agreed with the diagnosis and began a series of steroid eye drops, but it was only my eyes that received the drugs, as my parents did not trust the safety of ingested steroids. They believed that they could massage my joints, as my grandparents had done with Aunt Helen, and that I would be fine.

I loved to walk, despite the pain and instability in my knees, and my father feared that the walking was contributing to my joint problems; however, the doctor suggested that the walking might be contributing to my strength and generally good health and that I should not be discouraged. When my father did the grocery shopping, he would pull a wagon to carry the items home. I always wanted to go with him, and he would insist that I sit on the wagon so that he could pull me along, but there was no way

I was having it. I wanted to walk. The round trip to the Powers supermarket on Bloor Street took close to two kilometres, and it was no great challenge for me, even as young as three years old, and that was Dad's concern: that I was some sort of perambulatory mutant. Happily, the inflammation in my knees disappeared as the disease went into remission, and it was no longer an issue for decades.

CHAPTER 3

I am not certain how much thought my parents initially gave to my education. I was registered for kindergarten at the local school, Dovercourt Public School, which my brothers also attended. I was assigned to the smaller of two kindergarten rooms with Mrs. Davies as my teacher. I don't know how prepared she was to have a blind child in the class or whether she had any idea of how to deal with me, but I don't think it was the most productive year of my life. Peach had already taught me the alphabet using large plastic letters with magnets on the back to attach to a metal blackboard. I could spell the name of every person in my family, so playing with pretend food in a pretend kitchen did not hold my attention for very long. The food was made of clay and was supposed to resemble something I didn't recognize. And anyway, what was pizza? I knew that many of my classmates had an Italian background, but where was the good old Newfoundland salted cod or corn beef and cabbage? I especially disliked nap time. I wanted to be up doing things, so I just lay there counting seconds or listening for footsteps going along the corridor outside.

The one thing I can say to describe kindergarten is that the activities were all very visual. We seemed to do a lot of painting on large sheets of paper spread out on the floor. I, of course, needed a little assistance with colour selection, but by measuring things with my hands, I managed to trace out pictures that I believed depicted something. One particular piece of my art received a great deal of attention. My teacher graciously asked me what I was painting, and I explained that it was a red sports car. She confirmed that the black circles at the bottom of the page were the wheels. I have to assume that they were not approximated to the undercarriage of the vehicle and therefore a little abstract. Then she asked about the two pink stripes emerging from the top of the car roof. I was incredulous. Why did people who could see require so much detail to understand things? Those were the ears of the rabbit driving the car! Perhaps one had to be blind to understand this, but when a rabbit drove a sports car, the ears protruded through the roof! She was so enchanted by it that she wrote *Rabbit driving a sports car* on the page and put it up on the display board in the corridor for the school open house. Peach always laughed when she thought about the rabbit's ears outside the car. I wonder if this is how Picasso got his start.

I think the other incident that caused Mrs. Davies to shake her head occurred while we were playing a fishing game. Each child was given a fishing rod of a specific colour. On the floor were two construction-paper fish, each having a corresponding colour to the rod in one's hands. The rod had a string with a magnet, and each fish had a metal clip on its nose. The object of the game was to catch the two fish that matched the rod. Being of Newfoundland ancestry, I was excited about this game. I was told that my rod was orange. Supposedly, there were two orange fish on the floor, but there were also two blue, two green, etc. I dropped my line into the fray and caught a fish. Someone yelled at me for catching their fish, so I tossed it back. This catching and yelling sequence happened a couple of times, and so I stepped back and held up my fishing rod. The teacher wanted to know why I wasn't participating. I didn't want to say that I couldn't tell which fish were mine, and I didn't like being snapped at by nasty five-year-olds, so I explained that I would wait until everyone else caught their fish, and the last two would have to be mine. I think she shook her head. There is some sort of rule about five-year-olds not being able to analyze to that degree.

That first school year was not a total wash, as my nine-year-old brother Paul, who was a very good reader, revealed his sensitive, caring nature by going to the school library and asking the librarian for books that would appeal to a five-year-old girl. He would bring them home and read to me. My mother read to me every night before sleep, but she didn't like children's books so took me, chapter by chapter, on adventures to the South Pole or on a quest to win a pair of silver skates. Paul's contribution broadened my literary exposure to 1960s age- and gender-appropriate books.

I didn't just love walking—I also enjoyed almost any type of motion. Of course, as true Canadians, motion in the winter often involved ice skates. I started young, and with so many brothers and so little cash, my first skates were hand-me-downs from the boys. I dearly wanted a pair of girls' skates with figure skating picks on the front, but was made to be satisfied with a pair of boys CCM hockey skates.

Peach worried that I could get hurt if the other children at the local rink didn't know I was blind and that, if they did know, they might curb their activities and not have as much fun, which she didn't feel was fair. So each winter, Peach and Christopher would meticulously scrape the snow in our backyard and bank it up around the fences, leaving a flat base that they flooded with the hose every night until it was thick enough to hold their weight. Then they would go out each evening for two or three days, pouring kettles of boiling water over the surface to make it smooth. It was cold, hard work, but it meant that I could put my skates on in the kitchen and step out the back door for some safe fresh air and exercise. It was a good compromise, but skating around on my own while Ralph was off playing hockey with his friends made it a little lonely. Of course, Ralph could have skated there as well, but other children were not encouraged for the same reason I didn't go to the park, and hockey on my rink was absolutely forbidden.

After supper, my parents would be in the kitchen washing the dishes, and I would ask to go out on the rink. Dad would help me on with my skates, and away I would go, around and around and around. When my toes went numb, the pleasure of being outdoors would disappear, and I would go back inside with tears in my eyes from the pain. Dad would remove the skates and rub my toes to warm them up.

"I am never going skating again," I would whimper.

Dad would agree that was a good idea. However, as soon as my feet had thawed out and the pain was gone, I would ask if I could go out again. Back out in the cold, I would hear occasional knocking on the kitchen window—their way of letting me know they were watching me—which delighted me and took away some of the loneliness.

Summer brought other outdoor activities. Dad had a car for a couple of years and, on the occasional Saturday, it would be packed up with food, fishing gear, and the family in search of a river or lake. I was young and not yet able to read Braille, so I became quickly bored. I had my own fishing rod, but sitting with a line dangling in the water soon became too sedentary. I was often rebuked by my brothers for making too much noise and scaring away the fish.

Peach sympathetically encouraged me to sit still and be quiet, and she answered my whining protestations about fishing with, "You are part of this family, and this family is fishing today."

The result of my reluctant surrender was my discovery of the beauty of silence or, rather, the wonders in the sounds of nature. I found comfort in the water lapping against the rocks along the shore, the breeze rustling the trees, and the symphony of bird songs. There was also the softness of texture and fragrance in the dew of the morning contrasted with the harshness of dry, sun-baked grasses and bulrushes in the heat of summer. However, like skating around the backyard, it brought a little pang of loneliness, as it was not a shared experience but, rather, what I was relegated to doing while everyone else was enjoying something else.

Christopher was one of those boys who was never without a job or money in his pocket. He had a huge paper route and was often winning prizes for getting new customers. Having money meant he could buy just about anything he wanted, but he was not a spendthrift. He had his eye on a bicycle belonging to one of our cousins, and it wasn't long before it was his. He was the envy of the neighbourhood on his three-speed CCM racer. When not riding it, he would leave it resting against the railing on our veranda. He had a lock that he never used, as it was the 1960s, and people were still trusting. One day, the bicycle went missing, never to be seen again.

Paul, on the other hand, had a much more basic set of wheels. It had no gears, but was very trendy with its high handlebars and banana seat. He tended to leave his bike leaning up against the side of our house. Again, it wasn't locked, so it was fair game. This time, it wasn't a stranger who took it. It was me. I wanted to ride a bike so badly, I could hardly think of anything else. However, there was one problem: I was five, and Paul was nine, so there was a bit of a height differential. I could not sit on the seat, reach the pedals with my feet, and grip the handlebars all at the same time. Undaunted, I discovered that if I sat on the back fender, I could reach the pedals and, with a stretch, could just grasp the handlebars. With the most ergonomically inefficient posture, I somehow managed to teach myself to ride that bicycle. I would take it into the alley way behind the garages and ride up and down with the greatest feeling of freedom and independence. Then, Paul would notice his bike was missing and call to Peach, who would make me get off and put the wheels away. I would be instructed to not do it again, and I wouldn't—until the next time.

At the end of my kindergarten year, there was increasing discussion with my parents about where I would go to school for grade one. They had been told of a school in Toronto with a program for children with low vision, and they hoped that I might be accommodated there. However, Dr. Crawford broke the news that I needed to be registered with the Canadian National Institute for the Blind (CNIB), which wasn't available to children under six in those days, and I had to be sent away to the Ontario School for the Blind (OSB)—in Brantford. That meant boarding at the school from Sunday night to Friday afternoon.

As September 1966 approached, Peach began the process of preparing me for grade one at OSB by trying to shed a positive light on it as a place where I would learn to read and make friends with lots of other blind children. My parents were avid readers, and I embraced their enthusiasm; I was, therefore, excited at the prospect of learning to read. Sleeping there overnight and being away from my mother, whom I adored, was not so enticing. Never did it occur to me, as I begged Peach not to make me go, that her heart was being ripped out of her, knowing that she too would be away from me. Nevertheless, she insisted that I go in order to learn to read Braille. For, if nothing else, I would at least be able to entertain myself. Therefore, I had to go away to school, and I needed to be strong about it. She hung a cord around my neck with a key to the front door of our house. I was assured that I was going away to school because I had to and not because they wanted me to leave. The key was to remind me that home would always be home, and the door would never be locked against my entry. I felt enormously special and quite grown up, as even my brothers did not have a key to the house.

My family accompanied me to be registered at the school. We toured the dormitory, classroom, and playroom. Ralph was intrigued by the adapted toys, especially the rub, which was a large wooden bowl-like structure that spun on an axis. Three children would sit in it while a fourth child would kneel, one leg inside and the other outside, using their foot to spin the rub. Ralph thought that room a pretty wonderful place. We were buddies, and he, at almost five, had no understanding that at the end of each school day, he could go home while I had to go to that room instead of coming home.

The principal of the junior school, Evelyn Chorniak, informed us that going home on weekends was an option if my parents wanted it. Peach was very animated when she said that of course I would be home on weekends, as we only lived in Toronto. Sadly, Mrs. Chorniak had to admit that that wasn't the good fortune of every child, even some who lived much closer to the school than I, but Peach was adamant that I would be home whenever possible, and so began the regular routine of travelling to Brantford on Sunday evenings and coming back home again on Friday afternoons.

Initially, I was taken to and from school by bus, but soon that changed to my taking the train. After Sunday dinner, my father would take me on the subway down to Union Station to put me on the 6:00 p.m. train. I quickly learned all the names of the stations along the way as well as all the stops on the train, and I felt pretty confident that I could manage on my own if it ever became necessary. As if! On Fridays, the school staff would return me to the train that would arrive back at Union Station at six o'clock where Peach would be waiting to seize me in her arms and take me home. I have often wondered how my parents arranged who would drop me off and who would pick me up. I used to assume it was because Peach was so busy on Sunday with church, teaching Sunday school, making Sunday dinner, and getting the boys ready for school on Monday, but Dad was just as involved in all those activities. Peach eventually worked in an office downtown, and so picking me up might have worked better for her schedule. However, as I have grown to understand my parents more over time, I think my father understood how difficult it was for Peach to send me away, so he took on that role to spare her and left her with the greater pleasure of bringing me home.

CHAPTER 4

Although my time in Brantford was brief, lasting only two years, it was a lifetime to a small child, with experiences that have been a significant influence on me in many ways. It was the 1960s when the greater social conscience was in flux, and this school was no exception. It was rigidly structured with a strict schedule for everything from playtime to bedtime to toenail clipping. Of course, my home life was not without structure. On the weekends, I returned home for Saturday evening bath night and to sit down to dinner with my whole family, but it was different. Somehow, I belonged there, but I had to try and fit in at the school, and I don't think I ever truly did.

I was in the junior building for elementary school children, where I shared a room with five other girls. We each had a bed, a closet for our clothing, and a shelf for our toys. We were expected to make our own beds, and we were taught how to do so. At the foot of the bed, the sheets, blankets, and bedspread had carefully mitered corners. At the head, the top sheet and blankets were neatly folded back, and the bedspread was pleated over the pillow. I took great pride in making it perfectly. One day, while discussing something with one of the housemothers, which is what we called the dormitory staff, I put my hand down on someone's bed to discover that it was a lumpy mess. I inquired why that girl hadn't made it and offered to make it for her. I was told that she had made it just fine and I need not worry about it. But I did worry about it, and when I went to bed that night, I prayed for the housemother to tidy it up while we were in school. Even at six, I felt such compassion for that child who would have to climb into a lumpy bed because she didn't have the ability to make it any better.

My closet was sparse. I had enough clothing, but not an overabundance of it. I had one pair of shoes. Actually, I had two pairs of shoes, but one pair was for Sunday and, as I was home on the weekends, my Sunday shoes were at home. Since one can only wear one pair of shoes at a time, that should have been sufficient. Then I lost a heel in the playground. I felt sick to my stomach; out there in that massive expanse of swings and lawn was my heel, and I would never be able to find it. Fortunately, a visually unimpaired housemother noticed my predicament, retraced my steps, found the heel, and the shoe was taken in to be repaired. In the meantime, I was relegated to going about in my slippers, a pair of pink fake moccasins with a fuzzy trim around the ankle. I felt sheepish and very conspicuous as I sneaked into the dining room for dinner in my beloved moccasins that seemed to be betraying me. Of course, all the children were blind, but that did not matter. Blind children notice everything. I think the silence of my slippered footsteps spoke volumes. Fortunately, before long, I was happily stomping around in my Mary Janes once again. Soon after that, Peach bought me a pair of blue suede shoes with crepe soles that were just as quiet as my slippers, so I would never be found out again. Curiously, every time I put on those shoes, someone would call me Elvis.

My toy shelf had lots of space, and it was never difficult to find anything. Over time, I accumulated a few things, but not so many that it became untidy. Many of the girls had one or more musical instruments, and I longed for one. I was given a harmonica. It was small and inexpensive, and I loved it. I was no great virtuoso, but I could play any tune. However, the one thing just about every girl and boy had, and which I coveted most, was a radio. I undoubtedly mentioned a radio to my parents on weekend visits, but there was no way one could fit in the budget, and I knew it.

However, there was an elderly Irish woman at our church, Annie Greer. She was very kind to me and tried to make me feel better about going away to school by saying that only very posh young ladies got to go to boarding school. Even though she said this, I think that like my mother, her heart grieved for me. I discovered later that she had asked Peach if there was anything that I would like. Well, at home one weekend, Mrs. Greer gave me a gift. It was an eight transistor AM radio, complete with a leather case. It was not long before I knew every station on the dial and was singing along with Herman's Hermits and the Monkees.

Mornings in the dorm were always a beehive of activity with twenty-four girls getting ready for the day. I found the fragrance of morning very welcoming. The perfumed soapy steam in the bathroom mingled with the scent of toast wafting from the kitchen; however, once in the dining room, we were met with a warm bowl of oatmeal porridge or Cream of Wheat. That hot bowl of lumps, which we had four out of five days (Thursdays were left for cornflakes), was nasty stuff. For me, there is a reason gruel rhymes with cruel. Ever since, I have associated the smell of oatmeal porridge with wet flannel pyjamas.

Grade one was much different than kindergarten, and I loved it. It was a sort of adventure with new things to discover every day. We learned geometrical shapes that were cut out of sandpaper of different coarseness. Some were very rough, while others were rather suede-like. I suppose the purpose was to increase the tactile sensitivity of our fingertips in preparation for learning Braille.

The real excitement for me was when we learned that A is for apple. The next day, B was for boat, and I was off and running. I don't remember much about C or D, but I do remember the triumphant day that Z was for zipper. I was so eager that I asked my teacher to give me a book to read after school. She suggested that perhaps I wasn't ready to read a book yet, but I persisted, and so she gave me a volume of something, and I happily took it off to the playroom. As the other children noisily spun around in the rub or constructed houses out of Lego, I was oblivious, feverishly trying to read words—okay, a word or even a single letter.

When I returned the book the next day, I admitted that I was unable to read it. My teacher sympathetically acknowledged that she had expected this, but she reminded me that it was always good to try, and that I would eventually be able to read. I didn't feel discouraged, but my six-year-old mind was perplexed. After all, I had been on a twenty-six-day journey to conquer the Braille alphabet, and now that it was behind me, surely reading couldn't be that much more complicated.

While I was learning to read, my mother had acquired a book on Braille and a slate and stylus to produce it. It is a complicated method of writing Braille, as one has to punch out each individual dot and do it backwards, as the page has to be turned over in order to read the dots. Nevertheless, Peach taught herself the system, and every Monday, she sat down to write me a letter, which she would promptly put in the mail so I would receive it on Wednesday. This assured me that I was in her thoughts, and she believed it would shorten my week. As time is such a difficult thing to measure for young children, the period between weekends could certainly drag, and Peach's gesture was a very sensitive one. The letters were never more than a few simple sentences, but then my skills were not much better than hers. My teacher would help me make sense of the words, and I would hug the page once we were through.

One winter day, I was thrilled to hear that we would be going ice-skating. Apparently, they had constructed an ice rink on the school property, and there was a ski shed containing skis and skates for our use. Being more than a little curious, I stepped into the ski shed after my teacher to investigate its contents. It smelled musty and felt eerie, so I quickly stepped back out into the refreshing cold air. Nevertheless, I enjoyed the skating and wished that we could do it more often. However, the memory of that outbuilding and all the associated sensations were slammed abruptly into my consciousness one evening when I was in the dining room, of all places.

The dining room staff and cleaning staff were called maids. There was one, Annie, who was mainly responsible for cleaning but, occasionally, she helped serve meals. I admit that I was a bit of a picky eater, but then I was never very hungry, and food was more of a necessity than a desire. Mind you, there was not much to desire about the food at OSB in those days. It was 1960s institutional grub, prepared for the easy management of blind children. One can imagine this meant things were chopped, diced, and mashed. To me, it meant unappealing.

One dinner hour, as I was picking at my plate, Annie told me to eat my food. I protested that I did not like it. She replied that if I did not eat my dinner, she would lock me in the ski shed! I was gripped by fear, the musty smell now strong in my nose and panic rising furiously in my chest and throat. My overwhelming thought was that the shed was so far away that no one would know where I was or hear me calling.

Sometime later, on a weekend at home, I was eating dinner and, once again, picking at my food. Peach gently encouraged me to eat up, but without thinking, I blurted out, "Don't lock me in the ski shed!"

Sitting down beside me, Peach calmly asked me to repeat what I had said. I kept quiet, realizing what I had done, but Peach insisted. I plucked up my courage and explained everything about the interaction between Annie and me in the dining room. Peach hugged me and assured me that I did not have to fear anything because I had Mommy and Daddy, and everything would be all right. However, when I returned to school on Sunday evening, Peach accompanied me.

Once we arrived, Peach demanded to speak with Annie. She was told that Annie was not on duty. Peach insisted that they bring Annie in immediately. Of course, it was Sunday night, the staff were not in a position to do that, and Peach had to get back to Toronto. Absolutely furious, Peach left the school with these words ringing in the ears of everyone present, emblazing themselves upon my heart: "IT IS ENOUGH THAT THAT CHILD HAS TO GO THROUGH LIFE BLIND—she will not be threatened! If it happens again, I will plague Annie for life!" She spun on her heels and flew out the door with a determination that everyone understood meant business. It was never discussed again, but I have no recollection of any further interaction with Annie.

Although we always had some sort of dessert with dinner, there was little in the way of treats. When my father took me to the train on Sundays, we would pass the snack shop in Union Station. Money being tight, we did not stop. However, on one occasion, my father must have been feeling a little flush, so he detoured to the candy-, gum-, and chocolate bar–laden counter and bought me a fifteen-cent box of black liquorice nibs. My favourite! Feeling sorry for the children back in the dorm who did not go home on weekends, I saved my nibs. Once we were all in bed, I sneaked around giving each girl a nib or two. Suddenly, the housemothers appeared, and I was caught. Everyone was told to go to sleep except for me. I was seated on the bench in the corridor, where I was instructed not to fall asleep. A seven-year-old child being punished with sleep deprivation for sharing a few candies! This was a first offence, and yet there was no discussion about what I had done wrong or that I should not do it again. There was only punishment. What were they thinking? What a level of punishment for a blind child whose only crime had been sharing. I can still hear them laughing as one said to put me to bed whilst another giggled that I only lasted forty-five minutes, an eternity.

I never told my parents. After all, my father had bought the candy for me as a special treat, and I instinctively understood that the fifteen cents was a sacrifice; furthermore, even at that young age, I knew that if he discovered that I had been punished for sharing, he would have been heartbroken.

To suggest that everything at OSB was unpleasant would be untrue. The teachers were kind and encouraging and, although the students away from home, we were still part of life. As grade one was coming to an end, Canada was turning one hundred years old. Just like everyone else in the nation, we were preparing special events to celebrate. By then, my reading skills were developing, and I was given the task of reading a page of Braille that talked about the turtle being a symbol of life for First Nation Canadians. After practising reading it a couple of times, I had it easily memorized. Consequently, when my big moment arrived, I started reciting it. Two teachers quickly flanked me and whispered that I should read from the paper. They later explained that this was a combination of celebrating Canadian history and a demonstration of reading Braille.

Grade two was a very positive year. My teacher was Evelyn Chorniak, the junior school principal, and I loved her. She wore nice perfume, and her heels clicked purposefully along the corridor, giving her away minutes before she arrived. She was a no-nonsense person but, at the same time, she was warm and caring. She brought interesting things into the classroom: while learning about hibernation, a furry sleeping bat was placed within my hands. All I could think was, *I guess she couldn't find a bear.*

Like many teachers, Mrs. Chorniak had a good conduct program: if we met the standard of good behaviour and work habits, at the end of each week, we would get a star on our card. Once we had achieved ten stars, there would be a prize. Well, never put a challenge before me unless you are prepared to honour it, because a competitive spirit is always bubbling just below my surface. There was a boy in the class who was doing well with his stars, and the thought that he might reach ten before me was unbearable. After all, wouldn't the first one with ten stars be the teacher's favourite? It was close, but I won. The prize was more wonderful than a seven-year-old child, living away from home, could have dreamt: I was taken to Mrs. Chorniak's house for dinner. The menu, compared to OSB, was gourmet. I had a dish of alphagetti, a hotdog, and a dish of vanilla ice cream. To dine, I sat at an island in her kitchen on a high stool where my feet didn't touch the floor. Mind you, my feet wouldn't have touched the floor if I had been sitting on the rug.

One warm afternoon, we were not sent to the playroom after school. Instead, we were taken outdoors where a teacher was waiting with a bicycle. I was absolutely delighted to discover that I was going to ride that bicycle, although it was something I had never encountered before: a bicycle built for two. When it was my turn, I eagerly hopped on the seat, and we were off. It was only a brief ride, but it was marvellous. I begged the teacher to take me again, and I think he would have done so if he could have. He suggested that we might go again if there was time once everyone had a turn, but apparently there was not. Nevertheless, I now had a renewed passion. Once at home on the weekend, I excitedly explained to my parents that it was a bicycle with two handlebars, two seats, two everything. The person on the front does the steering and the person on the back just pedals and it is called a tandem. My parents' response was subdued. Perhaps they didn't want me getting my hopes up of getting one, and many times over the next several years, they would question whether I truly did ride a tandem in Brantford, but I certainly did. I had no other way of knowing about them, and as a child who loved bicycles, it was a perfect solution. But sometimes, exposing children from economically challenged families to new and wonderful possibilities can breed discontent, and I think my parents feared that happening to me.

In grade two, our class put on a production of Snow White and the Seven Dwarfs. Although I loved music, I had never thought of myself as an actress. I won the role of Sneezy. It was a musical, accompanied by a piano and with a little dancing. I, as Sneezy, had to dance around the other dwarfs lined up on the stage while singing something, perhaps "Heigh-Ho."

Everything was going well until my big moment arrived. The dwarfs lined up side by side and began singing. I stepped out and started skipping around the others. Unfortunately, the other dwarfs were also blind and had lined up too close to stage right, and as I merrily approached the last dwarf . . . Now you see Sneezy, now you don't! I fell off the stage. It wasn't very high, but I was only seven.

Not to be deterred from shining in my big performance, I jumped back on the stage and continued with the dwarfs singing away, feigning obliviousness to what had just happened. Now in some pain, I limped past the jolly troop until I came to the last one, which I grasped firmly and slithered around until I knew I was away from the edge. Suddenly, Mrs. Chorniak, who could contain her laughter no longer, put her head down on her arms across the piano keyboard, and the show was stopped by an enormous crashing chord. Needless to say, I have not pursued any other acting roles. Much later, when recounting this misadventure to CBC Radio's Fresh Air, the host, Jeff Goodes, suggested that the dwarfs should have been singing Monty Python's "Always Look on the Bright Side of Life."

Meanwhile, I had no sense of the discussions taking place or the plans being made that would forever change things for many blind children. One weekend while at home, my mother asked me if I would like to go to school with my brothers. I didn't understand, as my parents were constantly reinforcing the fact that I was going to school in Brantford to learn Braille and all the other skills I needed to succeed as a blind person. That hadn't changed.

"There is going to be an experiment," she explained, "to integrate blind children into the public school system in Toronto, and you have been chosen to be one of the first eight. This means you will not go to Brantford anymore after this year. You will live at home with Daddy and me and your brothers, if you want to, and go back to Dovercourt Public School."

I was a little bewildered, but excited, which was probably partially feeding off my parents' eager anticipation of the change in our lifestyle. In the meantime, the routine of weekly journeys back and forth continued until June.

Sometimes, one has to wonder whether certain occurrences are simply coincidence or an opportunity to reflect and determine what role one must play moving forward. Just such a day happened for me near the end of my time in Brantford, a day that has stayed with me ever since. Our teacher had been reading a few pages to us each day from the book The Miracle Worker, the story of Helen Keller. She lost her sight and hearing at about the same age that I had lost my sight, although many decades earlier. She was a devout Christian woman and staunch advocate for the use of Braille, and she fought for one standardized system for all blind people. Blind or not, one can only be inspired by her life of courage and witness. Interestingly, we read the last page of the book on May 31, 1968, and Helen Keller died the next day, June 1. The coincidence did not escape me. It was as though something important had ended and I had to know about it because, in some way, I had to carry on for her. At that time, 80 percent of blind people in North America were reading a universal system of Braille; was the integration of blind children into the public school system the next hurdle?

CHAPTER 5

I don't know whether my parents ever regretted having me at home full-time, but that first summer may have made them scratch their heads. Agitating for a bicycle, I was once again rescued by Mrs. Greer. She presented me with a little girl's bicycle, which I promptly mounted and was off. The laneway behind the garages was a great place for riding. Cars tended to mainly drive through early in the morning or at the end of the workday, so I could pedal back and forth with great ease all day long. I loved it. Unfortunately, before returning to school, I had an appointment with my ophthalmologist. Peach reported to him that I was doing extremely well, looking forward to going to school with my brothers in September, and always riding my bicycle.

Dr. Crawford practically needed a defibrillator. "Mrs. Vallis," he gasped. "Ruthy is blind. She can't ride a bicycle. She could get injured, killed, or kill someone else. You must take the bike away!"

"You heard the doctor," Peach said as she ushered me out the office door. My heart was broken, but I knew better than to protest, although the tears were stinging my eyes.

The bicycle was sold to another little girl for eight dollars, but I didn't stop agitating—I was good at that. Discussing a visit to the doctor with her brother George, Peach came up with an idea. Uncle George appeared with a big tricycle he had bought in a garage sale for three dollars. Peach and George were delighted to give it to me, but I was not so delighted to receive it. Tricycles were for babies, and I was not a baby. It was obvious that they were not pleased with my lack of gratitude. Peach had a tone of voice, like most mothers, which one instinctively knew meant business. She used that tone when she told me that I could take the tricycle or take nothing. Well, I wasn't going to take nothing, and I wasn't too bad at solutions myself. Tenacity was the mother of my invention. I mounted the tricycle and leaned to the right enough to cause the left back wheel to come off the ground. Ta-da! I had a bicycle. Somehow, I managed to ride that tricycle on two wheels. Adults would marvel while other children would say it was no big deal, but they never managed to do it. Eventually, I wore the tires down so much on the right side that one could not ride it on three wheels if one wanted to. Peach threw up her hands in resignation and hoped that I would soon get tired of the bike/trike. After all, she mistakenly thought, one cannot ride very quickly in that awkward leaning posture.

As Peach was working, albeit part-time, it was clear that I would be walking to school, occasionally on my own. Most eight-year-old children don't go wandering the streets alone, never mind blind children, but my situation was different. All the neighbourhood children walked to school, and it was understood that I would do the same. It just so happened that I was also blind, and it had to be accommodated. Consequently, I spent an hour or so each day during the summer getting lessons on how to use a white cane and maneuver back and forth from our house to school. It required crossing three small streets, one bigger street, and one main street with traffic lights. I managed it well and felt confident. However, I mistakenly thought that I would just walk with younger brother Ralph, as we were going to the same place, but he complained to Peach that having to walk with me meant that he couldn't have fun with his friends. Peach assured him that he was not responsible for me and was free to go and run. I walked on my own most of the time except for those occasions when Ralph decided we would walk together.

It was a long walk and, very often, very lonely. However, to ensure my safety, Peach went through all sorts of possible scenarios and grilled me on them regularly. She was not naive and, as a voracious reader, she thought of everything. I was not to talk to anyone nor be distracted by the promise of a puppy or candy. Furthermore, if someone said my mommy was hurt and they were to take me to her, I was not to believe it or go with them—just run away. The only safety net was Mrs. Greer. Her house was halfway between my school and my home, and that is where I was to go if I needed help. She was the only one authorized to meet me at school in an emergency.

September 1968 came, and so began a new adventure. I say adventure because that is how Peach wanted me to embrace new challenges and opportunities, including integration.

Much preparation was required for me to start grade three. Books had been ordered ahead of time, and those that were not already available in Braille had been transcribed. A teacher of the blind who had been working in Brantford, Shirley Lealess, was hired to work with me and other children also being integrated. Mrs. Lealess came every morning and took me out of class to teach me Braille skills, the use of an abacus for arithmetic, a Braille geometry set and, eventually, a manual typewriter for ten-finger typing. The rest of the day, I joined my sighted classmates, where Gloria Watson taught us all the usual grade-three subjects.

It was during that year that I learned the very important skill of telling time. For the sighted children, they learned to simply have the ability to be places on time or know when to leave, but for me, it had an even greater significance. It can be an important tool for navigation or relating perspective; when describing where food is on one's plate, for instance, people will often use the face of a clock and say that the chicken is at six and the peas are at nine. Some of my friends think they are funny when they say that the chicken is at ten past two or the potatoes are at a quarter to seven. Whatever the usage, telling time came in handy, but I became obsessed, and so began my agitation for a Braille watch, which was read by lifting the hinged glass and feeling the hands against the raised dots that indicates position on its face.

With the commencement of the integration program came a great deal of interest from educators, PhD candidates, and the media. Although there were eight children in the program, much of the attention was on me, and

Peach was concerned about it. She was adamant that my home address and the name of my school should not appear in any publication. Furthermore, one of the program directors had openly stated that if Ruth Vallis could succeed in integration, they would try other children, but if Ruth Vallis couldn't succeed, no blind child could. Peach was very distressed by this statement and did not want me to hear it. She felt it unfair to put the burden for success of a major new educational initiative on a young child. I, on the other hand, was unfazed. I did hear it, but I did not understand what it meant. There were lots of things that seemed to go over my head. I was commonly referred to or introduced as "a pioneer," but I could never quite correlate anything I was doing with the people who travelled across Canada in a horse-drawn carriage.

The media attention, although a little stressful for my parents, was fun. I was interviewed by a woman from the CBC. It was a warm afternoon, and we had a new tent pitched in our backyard, a gift from an aunt and uncle visiting from Newfoundland. I was rather more excited about the possibility of sleeping outdoors than the interview, so I invited her to see the tent. She feigned great enthusiasm and crawled inside, suggesting that the tent might be the perfect place for the interview, likely figuring it was the only way to hold my attention long enough to complete the task. I don't remember much of what I said, except that Paul was my favourite brother and I would like a Braille watch. I informed her that they were available at the CNIB Foundation for seventeen dollars. I was only answering her questions. I didn't give any thought to who or how many people would listen to my interview, but I soon learned that there were quite a few. Many people, strangers, offered to buy me a watch, but one anonymous person didn't offer; they just contacted the CNIB Foundation, and a ladies Braille watch was delivered to me. I was delighted with the watch, but at the same time bewildered by someone sending me such an expensive gift without wanting me to know who they were.

Several visitors came to our school to observe me at work and play, and I was also taken to meetings or other schools where I would talk about my experiences. I became comfortable speaking in public and enjoyed answering questions, especially if my answers made the audience laugh, although I wasn't always certain why. In December, an article was printed in the Toronto Telegram and was picked up by other newspapers all across Canada. My grandmother read it in St. John's, and my godfather read it in Vancouver. However, I became tired of hearing about it and just wanted it to stop. The attention started to make me feel different than everyone else, but the whole point of being integrated was to be part of a place where I felt I belonged.

My reading skills were improving steadily, so I took Kit Carson: Folk Hero and Man out of the Braille library and struggled my way through it. Unlike my brothers, I was not able to get help from my parents when I was stuck on a word or punctuation mark. They would try to make suggestions, but it was often more frustrating than helpful. Nowadays, there are books produced with both Braille and ink print so that blind children can read with sighted parents or a blind parent with a sighted child. However, in those days, that was unheard of, and as my frustration grew, my parents feared that I would lose my enthusiasm for reading.

Peach, with her crazy sense of humour, used to say that for every solution, there was a problem. This was one of those situations. She was determined for every challenge to be a stepping stone to success and not an obstacle for failure or surrender. She was determined that I would not be beaten and that everything was solvable. I needed reading practice, and she needed a way to know what I was reading so she could help me. The Bible! My parents read the Bible every day of their lives, and if I had a Braille Bible, they would know what I was reading and be able to help me. Aunt Helen eagerly sent me her Braille New Testament, and so began a bonding between Peach and me that went into the depths of our souls.

Every evening after dinner, Peach would sit in her rocking chair and knit warm outfits for babies living in remote parts of northern Canada and hats and scarves for the homeless of Toronto. Sitting across from her, I would read a few pages from a Gospel. We started with Matthew and worked our way through them all. Every now and then, she would stop me when we came to one of her particularly favourite passages, and she would explain it to me and why it was so extra special. In chapter 14 of Matthew, we read the very sad story of the beheading of John the Baptist. I was horrified by the brutal act, but Peach didn't want me to dwell on the event. Rather, she wanted me to understand what was behind it. She explained that the motivation for requesting John's head was jealousy, and jealousy was a very destructive thing. She went on to say that one's motivation for doing anything should always be love, and that I would later read in the Bible that in true love, there is no jealousy. I grew to love the Bible, the word of God.

My father was equally eager for me to have reading practice, and so he also found his own solution to assist me. He encouraged me to order a copy of Julius Caesar from the Braille library. It may sound odd for an eight- or nine-year-old girl to read Shakespeare, but it's not so unusual when one realizes that the King James version of the Bible and Shakespeare were written in the same language and that I had been hearing, and now reading, that language since birth. Words like thou and thrice were not unfamiliar. The story may have been a little beyond me, but Dad helped me along.

My parents were busy with work, home, and church, and so attending parent-teacher meetings for those who were integrated and the parents of those who may be integrated in the future was not a priority. However, Peach did attend one meeting and took me along so I could meet up with the others whom I knew quite well, some still attending the school in Brantford. We were sitting next to a woman and her daughter who were living a completely different life from us. The other girl was an only child, her father a university professor and her mother a stay-at-home mom. The other girl had not yet been integrated, although her mother very involved with the program.

The woman casually asked Peach what she was doing these days, perhaps because she never saw her at any of the meetings. Peach replied that she was doing the usual: working, family, and church.

The woman was horrified. She gasped, "You are not going to work with Ruthy in school in Toronto?"

Peach, completely unconcerned about what other people thought, didn't miss a beat. "Of course I am working! Ruthy is a part of our family and not the axis on which it revolves, and if she cannot cope in school and at home, then she will have to return to Brantford."

When discussing the interaction much later, Peach suggested that that was probably why I was integrated and her daughter was not. They had different expectations of themselves and their children. Furthermore, we couldn't afford her thinking.

With every choice in life, there are gains and losses, and whenever one makes a decision, one must always carefully examine what will be lost. My parents well understood my passion for music and knew that leaving the school for the blind meant the loss of a music program specifically geared to blind children. However, they felt that might be salvageable. They found an accomplished European piano teacher, the mother of one of my class-mates, who was willing to take me on. She acquired the basic piano books in Braille from the CNIB Foundation but, unfortunately, Braille music was not written like sighted music, and so neither of us could make sense of what was on the page. The musical notes were indicated by alphabetical letters, but they did not correspond. They tended to be offset by one; for instance, the note *C* was indicated by the letter *D*. She believed that, in time, I would learn to correlate what was on the page with that which was being played and somehow teach myself to read the notation. That might have been the case if I were a little more disciplined. However, I would come back for the next lesson playing the little piece, but then I would offer a variation in a slightly more creative style. I spent more time "improving" the piece than I did trying to perfect it as originally composed. A music teacher's nightmare. After only a few lessons, my parents were informed that my piano teacher's husband's job was transferring him, and his family would be moving to Thunder Bay, a twenty-hour drive north of Toronto. I hope this was true—I would hate to think that it was an elaborate plot just to escape me.

I made a friend at school, and the others in my classes treated me fine, but I took some verbal abuse in the schoolyard. Children would call me blindy or ugly, saying that I didn't know it because I couldn't look in a mirror. I mostly brushed it off, but when my brother Paul got in on the act, it was especially hurtful. I went home crying, and upon discovering me in a tearful state, Peach tenderly asked what was the matter. I was not com-pletely honest in that I did not divulge specifically who was involved, but I did admit that children were making fun of me, calling me a blind bat.

Peach stiffened. "I am sorry, Ruthy. It is a cruel world. Unfortunately, people will not always accept you because you are blind. If you are going to survive in this world, you are going to have to be tough! If they call you names, then you call them names right back—but try to be funny!"

It was not the reaction I expected from her. There was no hug, no stroking, nothing.

Many years later, when I mentioned the incident, she said her heart bled for me, but she knew that if she gave in to my tears, I would not have developed the strength I needed to be successful in a less-than-generous world. She knew it would always be hard for me, but she had to save the soft shoulder for when it really counted. Peach had a *big-girls-don't-cry* approach to life. She believed there was a difference between a female and a woman, and the difference was strength and courage. Ralph and I would bring home our report cards, and my marks were generally a little higher than his.

Peach would make a big fuss about Ralph's results and say, "Daddy, I think that report card is worth fifty cents," and the money would be passed over. I never received the same reaction. Peach would talk to me in private and make her comments on my marks, telling me "Well done" or "You could do better," and I would be given my fifty cents.

When I asked why Ralph got such a reception but I did not get the same fuss even though my marks were better, she would pat me on the knee and say, "We're women, Ruthy, and we don't need so much attention as men. You know whether you did your best, and you know that I love you."

I was not certain that I didn't want a little attention, but I loved that Peach felt we were different and strong as women and that we had each other.

I was always up for things that appeared adult. One day, during grade five, our teacher told us that she was going to the Art Gallery of Ontario on Saturday morning and we were welcome to join her there. Anyone interested was to meet her at ten in the lobby. I talked about it at home, but would certainly not be able to go alone, so my brother John offered to take me. I had never been before and did not know what to expect, but I felt quite proud that John and I were doing something so grown up.

When we arrived in the lobby, there was no teacher. In fact, it was very quiet with very few people at all. We waited for a while, but John suggested that we not wait any longer and that he would take me around himself. He introduced me to several pieces, but nothing made a bigger impression

34

on me than Claes Oldenburg's Floor Burger, a giant canvas hamburger with a pickle on top. I felt it thoroughly and identified it easily. It made art personal and real to me, a ten-year-old child. I fell in love with art that day.

Although delighted to go places with John, I loved nothing more than to do things with Peach when they didn't involve the rest of the family. She was very involved with the women's group at church, Action Line. They met on Monday evenings for an hour or so and knitted or quilted while discussing, planning, and organizing church events and fundraisers. There was always a cup of tea and a cookie and a whole lot of laughter, especially with Peach present. Occasionally, I was invited to accompany her. I loved it for many reasons. Peach was very popular, and I was proud to be her daughter. The meeting ended at eight thirty, which was thirty minutes past my bedtime, so it meant I got to stay up later, making it another one of those grown-up situations, and I also loved the company of women with all the energy and comradery. There was always a lot of chatter, and they seemed to achieve so much together. When I commented on it to Peach, she told me that there was nothing as powerful as women working together for good.

Peach's best friend, Grace, passed away when I was nine years old. It was a blow to Peach because they did so much together and were the founders and driving force behind Action Line. However, Grace's daughters kept in close contact with Peach and included her in some family events. When one of the daughters was getting married, Peach and I received an invitation to a shower. All the women there were the bride's age except for us, but as I said, Peach was so well liked that even the young women wanted her around. The popular topic of discussion at that time was the Equal Rights Amendment. Of course, the ERA came up at the shower, and the young ladies were all eager to hear Peach's opinion. She was very progressive, and I think everyone thought they knew what she would say.

She started with, "I don't believe in equality for men and women," and everyone gasped. "No," she went on, "I don't think women should lower their standards!" There was gales of laughter and applause. I only half understood what she was saying, but I was certain she was my hero.

By age eleven, I was fairly proficient at ten-finger typing and using a typewriter for all my tests and assignments. It made everything a whole lot easier for my teachers, but not being able to read back what I had written made it a little challenging. I would have rather composed things in Braille and had them transcribed, but that was time-consuming and cumbersome, and the typewriter was the best solution under the circumstances.

One of my grade six assignments was to write a poem. It was an autumn day, and I wasn't feeling well, so I lay on my bed while the neighbourhood children played outside. My window was open, so I listened to the calling, shrieks, and laughter that were so familiar and comforting. Depending on what the children were playing, I often sat on the sidelines and listened, unable to join in. It became the inspiration for my poetry assignment:

Hear the happy children playing, dancing up and down the street.
Hear the music of their laughter,
Hear the tapping of their feet.

I typed it out and let my parents read it. They felt it an adequate effort and encouraged me to turn it in. I was off school for a couple of days, but when I returned, I handed my poem to my teacher. He read it and asked me where I got it from. I told him I got it from my mind.

He challenged me. "Which book did you get it from? This couldn't have been written by you."

I protested with tears stinging my eyes, but he disposed of it in the wastepaper basket, and I was denied a mark for the assignment. I was afraid to tell my folks what had happened, and when they later inquired how the teacher had received it, I simply said that everything was fine.

CHAPTER 6

Discarded poetry was the least of my troubles during grade six. I had a much bigger issue, and this may have been my defining break between childhood and young adulthood. I was eleven years old when Peach took me to visit Dr. Crawford again. The inflammation in my eyes had long since burned out, and it was time to determine what was left and whether there was anything that could be done for me. Although I could not identify shapes, I could see shadows and distinguish colours. The doctor explained that I had a cataract on my left eye, but he believed that there was sight behind it, and if he could get it off, he might be able to restore some vision. He spoke directly to Peach as though I were not there, explaining that there was a fifty-fifty chance of success and the degree of possible sight restoration was a complete unknown. He then asked Peach whether she wanted him to go ahead with the surgery.

Peach turned to me and asked if I wanted the surgery. He protested, explaining to Peach that she had to make the decision, as I was a minor. One must remember that disclosure and informed consent were pretty much unheard of by any patient of any age at that time. There were people dying of cancer whose families would not let them be told the truth. However, Peach said, "Oh no, doctor, no one can make this decision for Ruthy. This is her eye, and only Ruthy can make this decision."

She then turned to me and asked if I understood. Peach laid it out very simply so there would be no misunderstandings, not that day nor any day going forward. "Ruthy, the doctor believes that there is some sight behind the cataract on your left eye. We can leave it there and go on just like we are now, and if that is your choice, we will accept it, and there will be no more said about it. However, if you say that you would like the surgery, then you must understand that there is a 50 percent chance that they may be able to save the sight behind the cataract, but there is also a 50 percent chance that they will not be able to save your sight. If you say yes, have the surgery, and it is successful, you will have only yourself to thank. But if you say yes, have the surgery, and it is not successful, then you will have no one to blame. Do you understand?"

I did and I said so. I was then asked if I wanted the surgery or not. I said that I did. The doctor sat silently, surprised at my mother's candour.

The date was set for me to be admitted to the Hospital for Sick Children on March 29, 1972, and the surgery was to take place the next day. Good Friday was on March 31, and Easter Sunday was on April 2. All in all, it was a very significant time in our lives.

As I was wheeled into the operating room, Dr. Crawford placed his hands over my eyes and said that they would do their best, but there were no promises. I didn't understand why he felt a need to say it again, as I had made my decision clearly, but I was aware of some trepidation on his part. Perhaps it was simply that, although Peach had signed the forms, he did not have the parent's consent but rather the child's, and he was unaccustomed to that. But Peach was right: whether successful or not, I was the one who had to live with the consequences.

I awoke from the surgery with a bandage taped from the top right side of my forehead to the left side of my neck and feeling very hungry. When the surgeon came to see me later, I did not complain of pain or even inquire whether I would be able to see. I just begged him for food. He insisted that he could not give me any food because I would throw up and, if I did, he would be in trouble with the nurse. I assured him that I would not throw up, but I might die of starvation. Twelve-year-old girls can be very dramatic, and it must have been an Academy Award-worthy performance, because he returned within an hour and handed me a hotdog, vanilla ice cream, and a glass of ginger ale. He cautioned me not to be sick and left. I devoured the feast and, true to my word, was not sick.

However, there was something going on, and he did not disclose anything to me. Peach wanted to speak to him to inquire about the surgery, but she was told that the doctor did not speak to family members on holidays. Nevertheless, she was eager to get in touch with him and so called his office on the off chance that he might be there. Somehow, the surgeon accidentally picked up the phone and agreed to make an exception.

"How is Ruthy's eye?" Peach asked.

"I am sorry, Mrs. Vallis, but Ruthy has the sickest eye I have ever seen." Peach began to cry.

"No, Mrs. Vallis. You can't cry now! Now is not the time for tears. You have been so strong, and if ever you needed to be strong for Ruthy, it is now." He went on to explain that normally, a cataract was soft like cotton wool, but my cataract had calcified and was harder than granite. "I tried cutting it off," Dr. Crawford told her. "I tried the laser and finally chipped it off in little pieces. Her eye haemorrhaged, and when I took the dressing off this morning, the eye was still haemorrhaging. We can't get it to stop. Ruthy may never be able to see with that eye. She needs your strength now more than ever!"

Peach told me everything. She explained about the haemorrhaging and that we just had to wait for it to stop. In the meantime, we prayed about it together. I received multiple messages that my church had prayed for me during the Friday service. Each subsequent day, however, the haemorrhaging continued. Although she was always encouraging and cheerful with me, Peach was desperate. She had explained the procedure and left the decision up to me, but she still felt enormous guilt that I was not aware of until decades later. Everyone we knew was calling the house and asking about me. My parents explained what was happening and requested prayers. Everyone in every church we knew had me on their prayer list. In fact, one of Peach's workmates was British, and she called a family member in England to ask people there to pray as well, and one of them lit a candle for me in York Minster cathedral on Easter Sunday.

I don't know whether that was what did it, but on Easter Monday, when they took off the dressing, the haemorrhaging had stopped. Gradually, I was able to see colour and even a few shapes again, but there was very little improvement, and it was not stable. I remained in hospital for nearly three weeks.

While I was there, Peach's boss—a wealthy woman in her own right who also came from old Toronto money—asked her if there was something I would like. Did I have a favourite fruit, for instance? Peach said that I liked nectarines. Although one can get just about any type of fruit at any time now, fruit was only available in season in those days except for bananas and oranges, which didn't come from Canada anyway. One day, a basket of nine of the most perfect, delicious nectarines were delivered to my hospital bedside. I was overwhelmed. I couldn't believe that it was possible to get my favourite fruit in April, and I knew they had to be very special because they were in a beautiful basket, and each piece of fruit was individually wrapped in paper and placed in a fluted paper cup.

I couldn't wait to show it to Peach. "Look, nectarines in April! How did she get them?" Peach explained to me that people with money could have anything, and those with money who were also classy wanted things for others, too. "She wanted the nectarines for you, and she made it happen."

Peach well understood how the other half lived. Her mother, Nanny Mercer, had been the private chef to the wealthiest family in Newfoundland in the early part of the twentieth century, and she had taught Peach all the social graces—how to serve a table, when to sit and when to stand, and how to address everyone and when. Peach had also worked for other wealthy people and understood them, but she never seemed to want to be them. However, that didn't mean she didn't want what they had for me.

There were two subsequent surgeries on my left eye the following year, simply to maintain what had already been done. I had some light perception in my right eye, but nothing more. There was never any improvement and, in fact, my vision was very slowly deteriorating. Peach's constant prayer was not that I would get my sight back, but that God would not let the light go out. She couldn't bear the thought of me living in darkness. However, there are many ways in which the light is revealed in our lives.

My older brothers used to date some of the neighbourhood girls. One such girl was Marie Rey. She and Paul spent time together when they were teenagers. I had to pass her house everyday on my way to and from school. Like most of the Italian grandparents in our community, her Uncle Mike would sit on the veranda and greet us as we went past. It was a natural safety net. Marie and I became friends, although she was about five years older than me.

On one of my visits to Dr. Crawford, he said to me, "You have a good friend." I didn't know to whom he was referring, and thought he may have meant Peach, so I just agreed. However, he went on, "I received a letter from a friend of yours named Marie. She has offered to give you one of her eyes." Apparently, she stated that if she could give me an eye, she would do so, as she would rather that we each had one eye and be able to see than her have two and me have none. We were very taken aback by the offer. Who would even think of such a generous gift to anyone? Certainly, both family members and strangers gave pieces of their livers or a kidney to others, but to give an eye! However, Dr. Crawford explained that when we used the expression an eye transplant, it really only involved the cornea, and I would require an entire eye. Scientists were making headway in the lab with frogs eyes, but like the spinal cord, once the optic nerve was cut, it did not regenerate. The offer had to be declined, but we likely would not have accepted it anyway.

In 1977, I underwent one last surgery. Dr. Crawford discussed with me, once again, the fifty-fifty prospect of removing the cataract. I, now almost seventeen, agreed to take another chance. When I awoke from the surgery, his surgical fellow was standing beside me. His bedside manner was less than gentle, and he gave full disclosure a whole new meaning. My procedure had obviously been a repeat of the first one, and I suspect it had caused a lot of frustration in the operating room. The young doctor said, "You have a great surgeon. Anyone else would have walked out, but he insisted on finishing the job himself. Everything that could go wrong went wrong!" He was very animated and held nothing back.

When I eventually spoke with Dr. Crawford, he said this cataract was even harder than the left one, if that was possible. There was no way to remove it but to cut open my eye and take it out like a core. The eye was stitched up with eight stitches, each half the diameter of a human hair. They went to great lengths to explain that until the surgeon's hand was under the microscope, they didn't even know whether he was holding the needle and suture. The bottom line was that any chance for sight in my right eye was gone forever.

By this time, I was going to my medical appointments on my own, as Peach had to work and I felt pretty independent. Furthermore, there are some things in life that one just doesn't want to share, and that may partially be because one doesn't feel anyone else will truly understand. Or perhaps one wishes to protect those we love. It was a few months later when I sat in Dr. Crawford's examination room for the final follow-up after the surgery. I was barely seventeen.

He sat close to me, holding my hands, and said, "Ruthy, it is time to accept that you will always be blind. If I could cure one person, I would cure you, but I have no control over that. I have never met a patient in all my career with your disposition. You have always gone into surgery with a smile and have come out of it with that same smile no matter what has happened, and you deserve better."

I protested that where there was God, there was hope.

"Yes," he said, "but I am not God. I am limited by the knowledge and skills that modern medicine gives me, and we still have a long way to go. Even now, we manage things differently than we did with you in the beginning, and if we had that knowledge then, it may have made a difference for you, but it may not have. Ruthy, you have had some of the most severe eye inflammation I have ever seen, and no matter what we threw at it, the little fire behind your eyes kept burning."

Nevertheless, I left his office with a feeling of defiant hope in the possibility of an eventual miracle.

In my late twenties, I had persistent eye pain, and it was felt I should return to Dr. Crawford, as no one else wanted to touch my eyes. Once I was ushered into the examination room, Dr. Crawford embraced me, asked what I was doing with my life and, with great emotion, he said how proud he was of me. He believed that I was destined for something special. He inquired about Peach and suggested it would have been nice to see her again. "Your mother," he shared, "is possibly the greatest mother that ever crossed the threshold of Sick Children's Hospital." It was quite a statement when one considers how many tens of thousands of children have been treated in that place, but there would be no denying it by me.

CHAPTER 7

With Dovercourt Public School behind me, I embarked upon the new adventure of Kent Senior Public School, a two-year intermediate school. It was a much farther walk and required crossing the very busy intersection of Dufferin and Bloor streets. Since my recent first cataract extraction and the slight improvement in my vision, I tended to navigate without my white cane. The thought now makes me shudder, as using a white cane is a twofold blessing: it allows one to perceive obstruction and circumnavigate safely, but it is also a warning to others that one does not see well. Nevertheless, off I went to my new school, feeling excited and very young lady–ish. We had homeroom for half of each day, and the rest of the day was spent rotating between various classes, including geography, French, and most wonderfully, music.

Besides what we learned in class, there were several extra-curricular music opportunities. My teacher was Diana Chiarelli, a sweet, very feminine-sounding woman with a lovely singing voice who immediately recognized my love of music and was ready and eager to bring it out in me. I was interested in her guitar group and choir. My brother John had a guitar that he agreed to lend me, and away I went to school with the newly treasured instrument under my arm.

My first lesson taught me the E minor and D major chords. Perhaps in keeping with my heritage but contrary to my religious beliefs, this allowed me to play along with the song, "What Shall We Do with a Drunken Sailor?" The second lesson taught me an A major and, before long, Tom

Dooley was hanging down his head, and I was off! My parents were delighted that I was finally learning an instrument and now very happy at school because of it. Dad would often ask me to get out the guitar and play him a little tune. I added a few Newfoundland folk songs to my repertoire for his listening pleasure. Peach bought me a harmonica holder so I could play the guitar, my harmonica, and sing all at the same time. Soon, she scraped up enough money to buy me my own guitar as well.

I also joined the choir, which taught me a lot more about music. Diana was an excellent choir director, expecting a great deal from her singers. She was able to extract a level of musicality from twelve- and thirteen-year-olds that is rarely heard in school choirs.

I knew Peach loved me and had faith in my abilities, but when an outsider believed in me, it took my confidence to a whole other place. Teachers are often held to a level of esteem reserved for few professions, and rightly so. When we consider the amount of time and energy that teachers put into children in their formative years, we need to recognize and celebrate the contribution so many of them make to so many young lives. Diana was that sort of teacher. She loved teaching music, and she was not afraid to love the ones she taught. She saw my passion for music and eagerly encouraged my creativity and, along with it, the joy that music brings.

In June of that year, the grade seven students spent a couple of days being paraded around to the grade-eight classes to meet the teachers. Grade eight would be an important year, as it was followed by high school and decisions regarding which stream of courses to enter, thus defining the trajectory of one's future. We met the teacher who was especially keen on math and a few other teachers, and then we went into room six. The classroom door was yellow, and I could see it. As one's vision deteriorates, yellow is one of the last perceivable colours, although I did not know that fact at the time. I wasn't that fond of yellow, but it got my attention.

The room-six teacher was Miss Marilyn Colhoun. She was a well-established fixture at the school, and everyone knew she loved English. Furthermore, she was a world traveller, bringing her slides of India and Africa into the classroom. Although a devout Christian, she was the one teacher who taught her classes about the ten major religions of the world. She inspired respect through knowledge decades before diversity was even a word on anyone's lips. Meanwhile, I found my way to the penultimate seat and listened as she read us a short story about a circus. Afterward, she explained that she liked the story but didn't like circuses because when she was a young child, she was taken to a circus where a trapeze artist fell to her death. I was thoroughly taken by that woman's voice, the story, and her personal interjection. She then walked among the rows of desks, placing a question paper on each one. As she passed me, I noticed her lovely, distinctive perfume, but when I told her I couldn't read the paper, she took it away again and suggested that I just listen to the questions, and when it came time for the answers, I could give them out loud. Although my competitive spirit was stirring with eager anticipation to shout out the answers, I was worried she was another teacher who did not know that I was blind and wasn't prepared to make any accommodation for me. Why else would she place an ink-printed page on my desk just like everyone else? I was perplexed. Of course, there were several grade-eight teachers, and none of them had acknowledged me with any special accommodation, but this one was different. I was already developing a crush on her, and she was the teacher I wanted!

When I received my report card stating I'd been promoted to grade eight in room six, I was delighted. I asked my classmates whether room six was the one with the yellow door and the teacher who read about the circus, and everyone assured me it was. I think I danced all the way home, but once there, my big brother John did not share my enthusiasm. John had been in Miss Colhoun's grade-eight class as well, and his response was, "Oh, not that battle ax!" He explained that Miss Colhoun had an expectation that every student would memorize two hundred lines of poetry over the course of the year. Apparently, the last few days of the year were upon them, and John was short—by 120 lines. Miss Colhoun informed him that without the required two hundred lines, John would not receive his report card. This could only be described as laziness, as John liked poetry and had a photographic memory. Anyway, he went home, found a poem with 120 lines, one or two words per line, and memorized it. It may or may not be a coincidence that the poem was entitled "The Donkey." However, he fulfilled his responsibility and went on to high school.

John's comments caused me some consternation. Had my instincts been wrong? No. This became a very important lesson in life for me. Never get anyone else's opinion on anyone before you meet and get to know them for yourself. Everyone's opinion can be prejudiced, positively or negatively, by many factors that may not have anything to do with the individual involved. We must have the confidence of our own heart.

Although feeling a little trepidation with John's words still ringing in my ears, I started grade eight looking forward to learning from Miss Colhoun. Unlike John, I had all two hundred lines of poetry memorized by the end of October. There were excerpts from Tennyson's "The Lady of Shalott" and the wonderful Hindu proverb penned in English by John Godfrey Saxe, "The blind men and the elephant," among others.

My affection for Marilyn Colhoun grew, and she responded positively with a gentle, caring, and encouraging manner. Acknowledging my love for music, she informed me of a Christmas cantata that she would be singing in at her church, Farmer Memorial Baptist. She wrote down the time, date, and directions on the back of an envelope and handed it to me. Of course, I could think of nothing else but how to get there. I talked about it at home and, once again, my big brother John came to my rescue, which was a bit of a surprise, as although he had been a very faithful church-serving boy, he was not all that interested in church at that time.

Nevertheless, the Sunday afternoon of December 23, 1973, arrived, and off we went together to a musical performance in a church that would change my life forever.

CHAPTER 8

Church had always been a big part of our family's life. We were Anglicans, and I had already been confirmed. We attended a small, rather poor church that, by the time I was a teenager, had no other young people besides Ralph and me. Our parents were devoted to it and took on just about every role but preaching or playing the organ. They were the caretakers for years, which always involved us children. We enjoyed it while learning a reverence for the house of God as well as the importance of volunteer service. Peach and Dad had such a reverence for that shabby house of God that nothing was too much to ask in its upkeep.

Peach was one of several women who were responsible for the care and set-up of the altar. During Communion, the celebration of the Lord's Supper, the purificator, a folded linen cloth used to wipe the chalice after each person took a sip, would be covered in wine and lipstick. Peach would bring the purificator and the altar cloth home for laundering. This was no simple feat. Peach kept a pan, which was exclusively for laundering the Communion cloths. She would soak them and then wash them carefully by hand. After wringing them out, she would lay them flat to dry. The water used for the washing was then poured out in our garden no matter what season of the year it was. Being a curious child, I asked why she didn't just pour it down the drain.

"Oh no, Ruthy. That water cannot be allowed to flow into a sewer. That water washed the cloths used in the celebration of the Lord's Supper. Communion is our obedience in recognition of Jesus's sacrifice for our salvation and we must never give it any less reverence than it deserves." Once the cloths were dry, she would iron them perfectly and roll them over cardboard tubes to keep them without crease or stain, just like His sacrifice.

I was very familiar with the Anglican Communion and common prayer services and could recite most of them without much prompting, but the Baptist church was much different. Most of the hymns were familiar, but the prayers were sort of unstructured, and one didn't always know when they were going to end. I rather liked the free way of worshipping and felt comfortable with the loose structure.

I started attending occasional Sundays with Marilyn Colhoun, and these attendances gradually became regular. I was happy worshipping with my teacher. Most of the people were friendly, and there were teenagers in attendance. Marilyn would pick me up at the subway, drive me to church, and drop me home afterwards. Deep in her heart, Peach probably would have preferred I stay an Anglican with her, but true to her belief that one's motivation should always be love and never jealousy, she encouraged me to follow my heart and, as long as Jesus was the head of the Church, I could worship anywhere with her blessing.

I was a pretty happy girl seeing Marilyn each day at school and at church on Sundays. I hung on every word she uttered and desperately wanted to please her, but I was not always disciplined about my studies. Given a task on a topic I loved, such as history, poetry, or music, I was focused, but otherwise, not so.

On one occasion, Marilyn felt it necessary to have a serious talk with me. Her words became imprinted upon my heart forever: "Ruth, I only want you to do your best. If your best is an A, I won't accept a C, but if your best is a C, I won't expect an A." There was a lot of freedom in this statement—the freedom to do one's best and to know it without having to live up to someone else's determination of one's best. So many people go through life feeling insignificant or as though they have failed—not because they do not do their best, but rather because they do not meet someone else's expectations that may have been more than their best and were, therefore, impossible and unfair. Marilyn did, however, punctuate her comments with, "but I believe your best is an A." In my heart, I knew she was right, and I owed it to love to prove it, although I was not certain whether it was love for her, Peach, or myself.

Marilyn assigned a few minutes each day for writing entries in a thought book. We were encouraged to note down current events or opinions, and she hoped we would get into the habit and continue on long after grade eight. I had already experienced a great deal for a young teenager, and she wanted me to capture it for posterity: "Ruth, one day, you should write a book about your life and call it *Love is Blind!*"

I selected my high school, Bloor Collegiate Institute, which was an academic institution with a good reputation. Leaving grade eight, however, was very difficult. By then, Marilyn was the centre of my world, and the thought of going from being with her almost every day of the week to maybe only seeing her on Sundays was more than my heart could stand. I tried to explain to her how I felt, but she gave me a *"there, there"* and assured me that I would meet all sorts of new people in high school and forget my old teacher. Perhaps that is what she hoped.

I was devastated and spoke to Peach about it. "She says that I will forget about her, but I won't," I protested.

Peach tenderly acknowledged my feelings were sincere and said Marilyn didn't know me like she did; Peach knew that I would never forget Marilyn.

Marilyn had taken me to movies and dinner on several occasions as our nice adult/child friendship had developed over the year, but come September, she seemed to be distancing herself. I still met up with her at church, but things were not the same. I had trouble focusing at school and struggled mightily with a fourteen-year-old breaking heart. Peach was not pleased. She felt that Marilyn had initiated and perpetuated the extra-curricular friendship, and dropping me like a hot potato was not okay. Thinking back, Peach was correct; however, Marilyn's situation could be, if not excused, at least partially explained. Once I was no longer in her classroom, we had little in common and, after all, I was fourteen, and she was forty-three. It is difficult to maintain a long-term adult and child friendship, as it is so unbalanced on many levels. Furthermore, most teenagers would likely have moved on. There were lots of whispers about me eventually losing interest in the church, which I suppose people thought would resolve things. There was only one problem: I loved Marilyn, and

I grew to love the church as well. I was never known for my patience, but tenacity was a different matter. In my naive mind, I would carry on and wait for her to have a change of heart. If she could love me once, she could love me again.

There were many very fine teachers at Bloor collegiate. Although Mrs. Lealess was long out of the picture, I still had an itinerate teacher, Bertha Wieler, who came to see me in school. Now she mainly came on an as-needed basis. She was also a well-qualified mobility instructor and, whether I liked it or not—and I didn't—she was going to improve my mobility skills with a white cane.

I was not one of those teenagers who believed it necessary to fit in, but I was tired of sticking out. I felt that every time I swung that fifty-four-inch white stick back and forth, it said, *I am blind, I am blind*, like an annoying pendulum. Admittedly, I was bumping into things and people and was at great risk of being struck by a car or falling down stairs etc., but unfortunately, the teenaged brain is not always rational. Nevertheless, I was not given a choice, thank goodness, and I begrudgingly underwent my indoor and outdoor white cane mobility lessons.

Miss Wieler taught me one of the most important lessons I have ever learned in my life, one that everyone needs to learn but few ever do. It was during one of those training sessions where I had to walk along Bloor Street with my instructor following at an unobtrusive distance. I stopped at a corner to listen for the traffic before proceeding across. A gentlemanly young man asked if he could assist me. I declined and went off on my own. Upon reaching the other side, Miss Wieler instructed me to stop, as she wanted to discuss what had just happened. She had gestured to the young man to inform him that everything was under control and not to worry. Then she laughingly informed me that he was very handsome and I may have missed a great opportunity. She reviewed what had occurred and asked me why I had declined his offer. I didn't think I could accept, as I was learning and had to do it myself. She explained that safety always came first and, as good as I was, I could still accept help, as it was an added safety feature. "Ruth, it is important to be independent, but part of being independent is knowing when to be dependent."

ZING! Suddenly, the white cane transformed from being a billboard that told everyone of what I could not do into a tool that assisted me to do the things I could, and to do them safely.

However, there are many challenges to independence in any number of situations besides mobility. One thing that is always difficult for a blind person is to be in a large room with a lot of people milling about. I have often wanted to go around a room greeting people and just being sociable on my own terms, but I am usually dependent on others coming up to me instead. Sensitive to my predicament, Peach developed a communication system for just such a situation. She would whistle softly two descending notes that meant she was looking at me. If I was performing in something at school or we were at a wedding or some other large event and, for some reason were not immediately together, she would whistle, and I would smile, knowing that she was there. It was enormously comforting, and no one else was the wiser. It was our secret signal.

One late spring Sunday in 1975, everyone was talking about what they were going to do that afternoon after church. Marilyn had recently bought a bicycle, and she and a friend discussed going for a ride together. I felt heartsick. First of all, they were making plans as if I were not there. Furthermore, I still dearly loved cycling and longed to be able to go for a ride as well. Once home, I moped around, feeling very sorry for myself. Peach asked what was the matter, and I tearfully explained that Marilyn was going for a bike ride and I wished I could too. Peach admonished me to stop moping.

She was firm when she said, "You cannot spend your life lamenting the things you cannot do. Find out what you can do and get on and do it. I am sorry that you are blind, but it is no one's fault, and no one should be made to feel guilty about it. Go up to your room, sit in the garden, read a book, listen to music, play an instrument, do something!"

Of course, there were lots of things I could do, but just like skating around in the backyard on my own, I enjoyed the activity, but it was lonely. I realize now that Peach understood, but she couldn't do anything about it.

The following Tuesday afternoon, I came out of school and, as I approached the sidewalk, I heard someone say, "Taxi, lady?" It sounded like big brother John, but in the cacophony of teenagers leaving a high school, I thought it was my imagination. Then, closer and more loudly, I heard it again: "Taxi, lady?" That was followed by the whistle signal.

Peach?

"Yes, honey, it is Johnny and me."

"Hop on," urged John. "It is your new tandem bicycle!"

Peach had noticed a tandem in the window of Bloor Cycle, an iconic bike shop just doors from my high school, and she managed the $240 required to purchase it.

Excited, thrilled, and delighted, I climbed aboard, and we were off. Yelling goodbye to Peach, whose smile could be felt for miles, we pedaled away with me drumming on the handlebars in absolute ecstasy.

John took me that day on the first of what would be many "smell tours" of Toronto. Somehow, he always knew where the most fragrant gardens were and would map out a trip that would take me past them all. He would say things like, "Madame, breathe deeply the fragrant linden tree." It added a wonderful component to our rides that only a sensitive man like John would consider.

Meanwhile at home, Peach, with her *for-every-solution-there's-a-problem* philosophy, had set up our house in a very blind-user–friendly manner. The milk jug was a different shape than the orange juice pitcher, and each shelf in the refrigerator was a designated home for everything on it. If I suggested that I would like a drink of juice, Peach would say, "Ruthy, you know where the glasses are in the cupboard, and you know which jug holds the juice. If you need help, call me. Just pour a little in the glass, drink it, and then pour more and repeat this process until you have had enough." She was determined that I be able to help myself, but that ended at the stove. I hung around the kitchen as she was cooking, but we had a gas stove, and she would not let me touch it. She taught Ralph at a very young age how to cook, and I listened during her instructions. I also listened to cooking programs on the television, but that was it.

One day while doing my homework after school, I was feeling hungry, and I realized that it was going to be a while before Peach got home. Then it would take time to prepare dinner. I figured that if I could put the meal together and get it going that by the time my parents were home, we could eat. I think it was my buddy Ralph who taught me where to set the button on the stove to get the required temperature. Anyway, I hatched my plan.

It was a cold and snowy day when Peach walked in the front door from work. She was late because of the inclement weather and was tired from working in a very busy office. Then she had struggled home among the masses on the public transit.

"Ruthy, are you cooking something?"

"Yes, Peach," I replied. "There is a stuffed roasted chicken in the oven and green peas, turnips, and potatoes, but I can't make gravy. Peach, can you make the gravy?"

Sweeping my skinny sixteen-year-old frame into her all-enveloping embrace, she said, "Honey, you are the gravy!"

I cooked dinner for us every day after school from that day until I went away to college, and the funny thing is, she never asked me how or when I learned to use the stove.

Peach used to describe us as two peas in a pod, and that was true on many levels. We had a connection that went beyond DNA. This was evident one Monday evening as I was going home after my regular weekly band practice, where I played the flute. Practice ended at six. There was no one else going my way, so I walked alone. Although I was good with my cane, I was not fast. I began to tap my way up the several blocks of Dufferin Street. It was November, getting late, cold, and drizzling. I didn't have any gloves and couldn't put my hands in my pockets, as that would have negatively impacted my balance, and I needed to hold my cane. There was a lot of traffic on the road, so the cars moved slowly, which made them quieter and somewhat eerie, but all I could think of was that the people in them were warm and dry and probably listening to the radio. I felt lonely. I tried to walk quicker, but it tended to make me stumble. I thought of the people in the houses. They were warm and dry and probably eating or watching television. I now felt very lonely. My hand was stinging with the cold rain, and my eyes were stinging with tears.

Once I got to the corner where I turned for the long stretch toward home, I heard a faint whistle. I thought it was a hallucination, and I tried to shake it off along with my now burning, stubborn tears. I heard the whistle again, but louder. "Peach?" I dared to whisper.

"Yes Ruthy, it's me," she said as she threw her arms around me.

"Oh Peach," I whimpered, "I am so glad you are here."

With a tenderness that defied description, she said softly, "I knew you needed me." She had walked a long way to that point. Likely noticing my red hands, she asked where my gloves were. "Oh, never mind that, just put my right glove on, and I will put my right hand in my pocket. You tuck your left hand under my arm and, away we'll go." With her usual rapid pace, she swept me toward home, and before I knew it, we had covered in about ten minutes a distance that would have taken me closer to twenty. Once the door was opened, the aroma of sage and an onion-stuffed roasted chicken wafted out to greet me. As I sat warm and dry, enjoying one of my favourite meals, I said, "Peach, honey, you are the gravy!"

Although I struggled my first two years in high school, things suddenly started to fall into place during grade eleven. I had failed grade nine math. In fact, my teacher suggested that I not even bother attending class. I was so frustrated by it that I wasn't going to argue, so I stayed away. However, when the next September came along, there was a new teacher in the math department, and she was a whole different kettle of fish. Hazel Huntington was a young, enthusiastic new teacher who probably believed she could teach anyone and wanted to do so. I sat there unhappily. When she asked me a question, I would answer it, but then she would ask me how I got to that answer. I couldn't explain to her because no one up until that point had ever taught me how to write down the steps to solving a mathematical equation. I did it in my head, and that was that. She explained to me that I wasn't passing because I got one mark for the answer, but all the other marks were given for the correct steps to get to that answer.

And so began my extra-curricular math lessons—at lunch, after school, whenever and whatever it took to get me up to speed. She started with simple arithmetic until she found where the holes in my knowledge lay and began to plug them up. I was so far behind that I had to achieve an 84 percent on my final exam just to receive a simple pass. I think Miss Huntington took a ribbing from the other teachers because she was the only one who believed I could do it and, in fact, she felt that I had a legitimately mathematical mind. Well, lo and behold, I received an 86 percent. Ta-dah! Miss Huntington talked to me about her desire to teach children with learning difficulties and wondered whether I thought she could do it. I thought indeed she could, and she left to go to another school.

I continued to take math through grade twelve but was discouraged from taking it in grade thirteen because it would require using a calculator and, although there were some talking calculators, they were not sophisticated enough for what would be required.

My math teacher thought I should be a stockbroker. My English teacher wanted me to be a journalist. One of the teachers said that she would pay my tuition if I studied for a degree in music, and the history teachers thought there was no doubt but I should study history.

I graduated high school as valedictorian but with no specific plans for university. I had taken steps toward starting a degree in economics with the thought of becoming an international trade analyst, but I knew that I would have to get grade thirteen math as, without it, my choices were limited. I decided not to go directly to university, although I had every intention of being in a program in a year. I was studying classical guitar privately and would be focusing some of my time on music.

I contacted the board of education and inquired about grade thirteen math correspondence courses. I was told that the CNIB Foundation library did have some correspondence courses in Braille, but there were five hundred courses, and the chance that the ones already in Braille would be grade thirteen math was pretty slim. Nevertheless, I called the library and was informed they had three courses in Braille, and they would let me know which ones they had. Well, lo and behold, one of the courses was grade thirteen mathematical functions and relations! In the Bible, Romans, chapter 8, it says, "If God is for you, who can be against you?" I contacted the man at the board again and gave him what I thought was good news. I was used to a certain amount of prejudice because of my blindness, but I was about to experience a whole new low. He said that he had looked into the possibility of me undertaking a correspondence course in grade thirteen math, but he had discovered it had only been done once before by a blind person, that student was male and, even at that, he was only able to achieve a 64 percent.

Clearly, for my solution, I had just found the problem—and he was at the other end of the phone. However, the board had just been contacted by a woman who lived in Kitchener, Ontario, an hour's drive from Toronto. She was a math teacher, currently staying at home to look after her family, but she wanted to offer her services to the board if they had anyone needing special math help. I don't know how good the man I had been speaking with was at math, but he managed to put two and two together. It was agreed that I, a mere female, would take the grade thirteen math course through correspondence and Frances Schantz would be my long-distance tutor.

Of course, Frances couldn't read Braille, so we had to devise a way to communicate everything. We decided that I would have to become proficient in math language. I would Braille out my answers, read them onto a tape, and then send that tape to Frances. She would mark my answers and send her marks and replies back to me via tape recording as well. This worked well, and we managed to complete the course, only having ever met in person once. Oh yes, and the mere female had managed an 85 average. Ta-dah!

I would spread all my books, Braille machine, and tape recorder all over the living room floor while studying. I needed space, and this worked best. That is where I was sitting in January 1981, working on my math, when I heard a voice as clear as if someone were sitting beside me. The voice said, *physiotherapy*. I was startled by the clarity, but not fearful. I knew I was alone in the house, but I was certain about the voice. I immediately went to the phone and called the CNIB Foundation Rehabilitation Services department. I spoke with Boyd Hipfner, a very experienced rehabilitation counsellor. I asked him what he knew about physiotherapy. He said there was a physiotherapy school in England for blind and visually impaired students. I asked how to apply for the program, and he put the application in the mail immediately.

CHAPTER 9

I didn't discuss going to school in England with my parents until I had sent in my application. It is not that I thought they would discourage me, but I felt so compelled to do it that there was no use talking about it until I knew that it was a possibility. There were six students applying from Canada that year, and we were subjected to a series of tests and interviews over the course of a week. Although the University of Toronto would not accept me into their program because I was blind and they could or would not accommodate me, they had to be a part of the assessment to determine whether I met their academic standard.

We went through mobility tests that were not difficult for me, as I was already travelling back and forth each day for the examinations and using the subway and bus. The others also did well, as they were not totally blind, just had low vision. We had physical fitness tests and were taught some basic physiotherapy skills, such as measuring for and adjusting crutches and tensor bandaging. I had no difficulty with any of these practical tasks.

One of the final tests was spatial awareness, which determines a person's ability to know where they are relative to other things in space. This is a skill that everyone either has or does not have. One may be able to learn some adaptive tricks, but for the most part, it is not learned. This may be why some people are unable to parallel park.

My spatial awareness tests were twofold. First, I was taken to an empty auditorium with my back placed against the middle of a long wall. I was then taken to four places in the room that were referred to as one, two, three and four. These four points were evidently the corners of a square, but they were somewhere in the middle of the auditorium. There were no landmarks, that is, no walls, no furniture, nothing that I could touch. I discovered later that there were painted marks on the floor that my examiners could see. I was then taken back to the original place against the wall and handed four two-inch wooden blocks. I was then instructed to put one block on each of the four places. I did so and returned to the wall. I had no idea how close I was to the four designated spots, but I was not concerned about that until they instructed me to go to where I had placed block two, pick it up, and put it on top of block four.

Under my breath, I muttered, *"What? Are you kidding? Are you nuts?"* Nevertheless, I walked to the imaginary two, put my hand down, and voila! There it was. I picked it up and took it to block four, and there it was. Interestingly enough, that spatial awareness test was dropped soon after that, as there has been only two totally blind physiotherapy candidates to ever pass it: a very capable blind man from South Africa and me.

The second test was much easier. They placed four chairs to create the corners of a room and, on three sides, they placed a skittle (like a bowling pin) between the chairs to indicate walls. We were given different tasks that had to be completed in the little room without knocking over the precariously-balanced skittles. That was much easier. At the end of the week, there was an interview board, and then we parted company to await our acceptance or rejection letters.

After the first day of testing, I came home to dinner, and Peach asked me to feel around my plate. I did so and discovered a little box.

"What is this?" I inquired.

"Open it and see," she said, smiling. It was a ring. The design, she explained, was a V with five diamonds. "Ruth, this is to signify V for victory over your disability. Whether you get accepted into physiotherapy or not, you have conquered your disability, and you are a successful woman."

The letter came bearing the good news, and so began the preparations—getting a student visa, passport, and airline ticket, and, of course, packing and shipping. There were three of us accepted. There was Sylvie, a French-Canadian girl from Hearst, way up in Northern Ontario, and Gillian, from down the highway in Kingston. Sylvie had good limited vision and Gillian less so, but both read ink print and not Braille.

There were several people gathered at the airport to say goodbye to all three of us. Peach took me aside to speak to me privately. "Ruthy, I would like a few minutes alone with you before you go. I want you to know that tonight, I am sending to England all I have ever wanted and more, but this is something you must do for yourself. Study hard, learn what you must learn, and come home with your qualification. Don't let anything stop you. If I become sick, have a heart attack, or die, there is nothing you can do about it, so you must not come home. You must stay, think of yourself, and do this for you and your future. But Ruthy, remember you are a guest in that country. Keep your ears open and your mouth closed. Listen and learn, and say nothing." She hugged and kissed me, and I joined the others to board the plane.

Gillian's parents were from Scotland, and most of her relatives still lived in Britain. Fortunately, she had an aunt and uncle, Margaret and Eric, who lived in Kent, and graciously, they had agreed to meet us at the airport and deposit us at the school. It was a very warm Saturday in September 1981 when we arrived at the North London School of Physiotherapy for the blind and visually impaired. Although the school had been established in 1899 and until recently had been known as the Royal National Institute for the Blind School of Physiotherapy, it was now housed in a modern building in Highgate, North London. Upon our arrival, we were given keys to our rooms and the students' entrance of the building. The bursar showed us to the residence, and that was it until Monday morning. There was no orientation to the school or the community. I was twenty-one, blind, knew no one, and had basically just dropped out of an airplane into bustling London to embark upon a very challenging course of physical medicine study. Mommy!

My room was comfortable and up on the sixth floor with a window overlooking the accident and emergency entrance of the Whittington Hospital on Highgate Hill. I, thankfully, had a single room with a bed, desk, table, and chair, lots of cupboard space, and a wash basin. There were five other single bedrooms in our unit, and we shared two toilets, a bath, a shower, a kitchen, and a sitting room. We were expected to shop for our own groceries and prepare our own meals, but we could also eat in the hospital canteen when it was open. But there was a very narrow window for lunch and dinner. Bedding and towels were provided, but we were to do our own laundry. Of course, cooking and laundry were no issue for me, but without orientation to the community, I was stranded.

By Sunday afternoon, the other students started arriving, and some of those who were back for their second or third year invited us to the hospital for dinner. I was pretty hungry by then, thirty-one hours after arriving, so I agreed to join them. The menu was bangers, onions, peas, and roasted potatoes with gravy. Sausages were one of my favourite foods. For the record, hospital bangers do not qualify as sausages. They were filled with bread, not meat, and tasted nasty. The onions were barely cooked, the peas soft, the potatoes hard on the outside, and the gravy had no flavour. I was back to picking at my food. It may not have been easy, but one of the important passages from my childhood to adulthood was learning to drop any of my preconceived ideas. One must learn not to expect the familiarity of home everywhere one goes. No, the bangers were not to be compared with the sausages at home in Ontario, the land of pork. But there were wonderful sausages in England, and one could grow to love bread-filled bangers, and I did. In the meantime, I went hungry for a few more days.

Eventually, someone showed me how to get to the Co-op to buy my groceries. They didn't accompany me to help me select them, but simply gave me directions and sent me off on my own. It has been said that Canada and England are two nations divided by the same language, and that was certainly true for me.

After one week in London, I went off, armed with a grocery list, to purchase some necessities. I was determined for this adventure to not conquer me. Although this was a school for blind and visually impaired people, I was the only one in my class of thirteen who was totally blind. In fact, there was only one blind person in the second year and two in the third year. We were in a great minority, and those with low vision did not understand any more and, in many ways, were less accommodating or sympathetic than the normally seeing public. I mistakenly thought that there would be some help to get me settled, but every hour of every day involved some sort of discovery.

Upon entering the supermarket, I stood in one spot in the hopes that someone would notice me and offer some assistance. Eventually, I drew someone's attention. I asked for some laundry powder.

"Pawdon?" That was "pardon" to a Canadian's ears.

"Laundry powder?"

"Pawdon?"

"Laundry detergent to wash clothes."

"Oh, you mean soap flakes."

"Yes, I guess I mean soap flakes."

"Which brand of soap flakes would you like?"

My brother Christopher worked for Lever Brothers, which I knew was a British company, so I said, "Sunlight."

"Pawdon?"

"Why don't you tell me which brands you carry, and I will select one?"

"We have Persil."

"That will do. I will take Persil." Bread and milk all went well, but then I asked for the feminine hygiene products.

"Pawdon?"

Oh, not this again! I was puzzling over how to explain when another customer said, "I think she wants Lil-Lets."

I agreed, and a small box was popped into my hand. It wasn't quite what I wanted, but I took it. I actually wanted sanitary pads, which I later learned were known as sanitary towels. Who knew?

Nevertheless, our last stop was the cheese counter. Aha, I loved cheddar, and I knew Cheddar Gorge was in England. I am ready! I got this one! When the woman behind the counter asked what I would like, I confidently said, "Cheddar, please."

"Do I detect an accent, and would it be Canadian?"

I admitted it was.

"Would you like Canadian cheddar? It is our bestseller!"

Not wanting to surrender, I snapped, "No, I want English cheddar!" However, after that, I usually bought Canadian cheddar. It was, after all, nice to have a little of home away from home.

Taking my things back to the residence, I decided to do some laundry. There was no one else in the laundry room, so I read the Braille instructions on the machine, popped my washing in, poured the required amount of Persil into the receptacle, pushed a ten pence piece into the slot, and pressed the button. The machine started up, and I returned to my room to study while the clothes were going around.

Once I felt the washing was likely finished, I returned to the laundry room to find the residence manager mopping up bubbles that were waist-deep on the floor. It was like something out of a science fiction movie—the attack of the Persil bubble people.

"Ruth, are these your clothes in the machine?" he asked.

"My clothes are in one of the machines," I admitted.

"There is only one machine being used, so it must be yours. You have used too many soap flakes and have made a mess of the whole room!"

I protested that I'd simply followed the instructions written on the machine. After I held up my box of Persil to show him, he sighed. "Ruth, those aren't soap flakes for automatic electric washing machines. Those are soap flakes for hand washing. You can't put that in the machine, as it will cause all these bubbles."

How was I to know that many people in England still washed by hand? I assured him that I would ask for automatic soap flakes in the future and left him to clean it up. I couldn't imagine anyone not having an automatic washing machine. Why did the woman at the supermarket assume I washed my clothes by hand? Did I look like a pioneer?

I wanted to do well, and so I studied constantly. We had a test in one of our subjects every week. Our first test was on the anatomy of the humerus. I felt pretty confident, but once the marks were posted in ink print for everyone to see—except me, that is—I had scored only five out of ten. Someone had managed a ten. I was devastated. Discouragement was starting to set in.

To add even more discomfort to my situation, one of the lecturers, vice-principal Marshall, made fun of my accent every time I asked a question. During physics class, I said *leever* and *lev-verage,* but he corrected my supposed inconsistency to *leever* and *leeverage.* He instructed that if I was going to live in England, I should learn to speak English.

I retorted that it was just like *private* and *privacy,* which he always said as *private* and *priv-vacy.*

I do believe he snorted, "Touché."

He could read Braille, so he allowed me to write my tests in Braille, but then he criticized me for using American Braille instead of British Braille, which was slightly different but very understandable in both systems.

I also managed to find disapproval from another lecturer, Mr. Field. We were learning how to set up pendular suspension—the use of pulleys and inclined planes to facilitate or resist movement. Unaware, apparently, I was singing as I worked.

"Miss Vallis," Mr. Field snapped, "physiotherapists don't sing!"

"Sir, when I am qualified, I shall be known as the singing therapist."

"Yes," he snarled, "and you shall be fired in your first week for insubordination!"

Come Sunday, I wanted to attend church. I inquired about local churches and was told that Upper Holloway Baptist Church was straight down Holloway Road. The directions seemed straightforward. I was to walk down Highgate Hill, which led to Holloway Road. The church was on the same side as the school, just a few blocks down. Feeling fairly confident, I ventured out. I walked down Highgate Hill and straight into a wrought iron fence. I backtracked to the school and started out again. There was that fence again. Had I veered off? Was I on someone's private property? I reversed my steps again and tried it a third time. I trailed back along the fence to find the beginning and tried to go around it. No, I couldn't do that, as it was along the edge of the road, and I would be stepping off into traffic. There was no one else around, so I couldn't ask anything of anyone. I was forced to surrender and return to my room.

Back home, as it were, I became very angry. I yelled at God. *I thought you called me here. Why is everything so difficult?* I beat my pillow against the wall repeatedly asking, *Why, why, why? I don't know where anything is. I don't know the names of the products I need to buy. I can't do laundry without drowning in bubbles. I am stupid in school. I have the wrong accent. I use the wrong system of Braille, and I can't even go to church to worship You, and I am not even certain why I want to.* The rest of the day was spent sobbing or yelling at God.

I learned that the fence was there to keep people from crossing the road at that point, as it was a multi-directional roundabout. If I wanted to walk down Holloway Road, I would have had to go down into a pedestrian subway, which was a series of passages under the street. It would have required knowing which passage to take as well. How was I supposed to know that? We didn't have fences along the sidewalk in Toronto, and a subway involved a train. A tube was a pipe or piece of hose.

As I went through the motions of the subsequent week, home sickness started to set in. I went to my classes every day, but when I opened the door to my room in the evenings, emotional pain would seize me. I truly believe that if a person could die of home sickness, I would have been long-since buried. Eventually, I could take the pain no longer and called Peach. Through breath-halting sobs, I told her everything was a struggle and, on top of everything else, I wasn't making friends.

True to form, she said, "Ruthy don't forget that your best friend is always with you, and if you want to come home, then you do so. There will be no questions asked and no comments made." Of course, Peach felt desperate being so far away from me and knowing that I was so unhappy. She called Marilyn for some advice on what to do. The next thing I knew, I was being summoned for a long-distance phone call.

The voice said, "Ruth, it's Marilyn. I am very disappointed in you. Your Mother is frantic. Grow up!" Click.

Well, now I had something else to add to my list—it seemed no one except Peach cared about me.

Under my window was a large counter that was an extension of my desk. I stood on the counter with only a single pain of glass between me and the street six stories below. I wondered whether I would die if I fell or only become a quadriplegic. I just felt so alone and painfully unhappy. I yelled at God again and then remembered Peach. She had no idea what I was thinking and would never get over it if I hurt myself. She, of all people, didn't deserve that. I got down off the counter, fell onto my bed, and had a very serious talk with God. It was a Thursday, and what I said to Him was this: *I believe that you want me here, but I am so unhappy that if I do not start feeling better by Tuesday, I am going home on Wednesday!*

I awoke on Friday morning with that same sickening feeling. Entering my room in the evening, I could do nothing but lie on my bed and sob. The other students were becoming very aware of my unhappiness. The totally blind lad in second year came to talk to me.

He said, "I know you are homesick. You are very lucky."

Was he kidding? Had he any idea of what I was going through?

He went on: "I know you think that is a strange thing to say, but Ruth, I was sent away to a school for blind children from the age of four. I have never lived at home since. My family are strangers and, therefore, I don't have a home to be sick for. I would love to have a place to miss or people who missed me." It was kind of him to talk to me, but it didn't change anything.

On Saturday morning, I awoke feeling even worse, and I didn't have the distraction of classes to help me. However, I did receive a phone call from a friend of Marilyn's, Barbara Cherry, who lived in South London. She was coming up to Highgate to see me. Apparently, she had received a telegram from Marilyn that indicated I was in despair. Upon her arrival, she, too, felt it necessary to tell me to grow up and stop worrying my poor mother. She took me out for a meal and, once we were back at the school, she stated that I was better than she had expected, as she thought, from Marilyn's telegram, that I might be suicidal. I said nothing.

On Sunday morning, I did not feel any better, and I told God, in no uncertain terms, that I was not going to church and repeated that, if I did not feel better by Tuesday, I was going home on Wednesday.

On Monday morning, I awoke feeling even worse, if that was possible. I could hardly function, being racked with overwhelming physical and emotional pain. I couldn't eat, concentrate, or interact with others. I did go to my classes, but once back in my room, I could only lie on my bed and sob. I reminded God that tomorrow was Tuesday, and that there was no way I could possibly feel better (as I was worse than ever). So, I was sorry, but I would be going home on Wednesday. After all, if He had wanted it to work for me, He would have made it easier.

Like every other night, I cried myself to sleep. On Tuesday morning, I did my usual routine and went off to class. After school, I returned to my room and prepared to go to dinner. It was only then that it dawned on me: I had gone through the whole day and not thought of home once. The pain was gone. The sickening feeling was gone. It was Tuesday, and I felt better.

I yelled at God again. *I told you I was going home. Why have you made me feel better?* It was then that I heard that same voice, the one that said *physiotherapy*. It said, *I called you!* I went to the phone, called Peach, and let her know that I was feeling better.

The school had something called personal tutors. These were staff members assigned to students to discuss personal issues. My personal tutor was Mary Winter. She did some teaching at the school, but her main responsibility was to oversee students while in clinical placement with out-patients. She was a little like Peach—large in stature and strong but soft. She was obviously made aware of my difficult emotional state and gently offered to be a soft shoulder if I felt I needed one. Mrs. Winter assured me that her shoulder was large and could take a lot. She had also lived in Ontario for a year on exchange with her husband, who was a public (that is, private) school teacher. She would make me smile with comments about wind chill that no one else understood. I was not the type to talk to strangers, or anyone else, for that matter, about my personal issues, but I was glad she was there, and we did eventually become close.

CHAPTER 10

Money was very tight while I was in England. The exchange rate was $2.45 for one pound; consequently, my funds did not go far. I was very careful anyway, but I had to be especially so, as I learned I had to be out of the school over Christmas and, not having anywhere to go, I had planned to go home. Ralph was a professional soldier in Princess Patricia's Canadian Light Infantry. Knowing that the dollar exchange rate was so high and that I was struggling a little, he arranged with the paymaster to have fifty dollars garnished from his wages each month and sent directly to me. It was a generous gesture and an enormous help. Ralph explained later that he was inspired by what Peach had always said to him: "One should never go out without something in one's pocket." He feared that if I had no money, it would only magnify any other difficulties I might be having.

The least expensive flight I could find was on Laker Airways. I had to leave class early on the last day in order to catch that flight. One of the lecturers made it known that she was not in agreement. She felt it unacceptable that foreign students should get any special privileges over the British students. Of course, the British students all went home on the weekends where their mothers cooked for them, did their laundry, and often sent them back with care packages for the week. I didn't get that privilege, and neither did she invite me to her flat for a change of scenery. Fortunately, the principal felt differently and, as he knew I had been struggling, he was eager for me to get home for a break. Of course, that teacher gave me an assignment to complete while home to make up for my half day missed; some people love power.

I found that first Christmas vacation very stressful. The course was intense, and settling in had been so difficult that, now at home, I seemed to have a whole lot of pent-up energy. I wanted to be there, but I also wanted to be in England and get on with the course. I was delighted to see Peach and my family, but suddenly I wasn't a little girl anymore, and Peach's expectations of me and my expectations of her had to evolve.

I also saw Marilyn, which delighted me. She admitted that her stern words over the phone had not been appropriate, but all was forgiven, as I had gotten over it by then. However, unlike Peach and me, we were ready to evolve into an adult friendship. Marilyn had taught in England for a year, and we now had living in London to add to our growing list of things we had in common.

On Saturday, January 2, 1982, I boarded the Laker flight back to London. Seated beside a nurse, we chatted briefly and then settled in for the journey. The crew announced that dinner would be served shortly and, prior to dinner, they would be offering a cash bar service. It was a full flight with around four hundred people. Suddenly, I noticed things went very quiet. I commented on it to the nurse, but she didn't seem to understand what I was referring to. I said, "The engines, the hum and vibration of the engines."

Yes, she admitted that things had become quiet, but she hadn't noticed. Then the flight attendants started moving quickly through the aisles, offering drinks. The nurse asked for a gin and tonic, and she was given two. I asked for a ginger ale, and I also was given two. Thinking this was very peculiar, I asked the nurse whether she felt something might be wrong.

"It is odd," she said, "that they gave us two drinks instead of just one."

"Furthermore," I added, "they said they would be offering a cash bar service, but neither of us was asked for money."

"I think you are right. There is something wrong."

After a few minutes, the captain came on the PA system. "Ladies and gentlemen, we have lost ten thousand feet in altitude and half of our fuel, but we do not know why. We will keep you informed as we proceed." After a few more minutes, the captain informed us that they had discovered that the landing gear was in a mid-retracted position. They were unable to get it to retract any farther. "We will be making an emergency landing in Bangor, Maine, as we have gone too far to turn back to Montreal. Please fasten your seatbelts. Pay close attention to the seatbelt sign, and as soon as it is extinguished, release the buckle immediately and prepare to disembark quickly if instructed to do so. We do not know whether the landing gear will go down into place, and we will not know until it is time to engage it."

I asked the nurse to keep me informed regarding the seatbelt sign.

I am not sure whether one can surmise how a plane full of people react in these situations, but I can tell you that most of the passengers on that flight were British folks returning home after a Christmas vacation in Canada. There was a collective stiff upper lip that left the aircraft in complete silence. Perhaps everyone was praying or just holding their breath. I sat back and asked the Lord to take the plane into His hands, and time stood still.

We seemed to be floating. The nurse said she could see emergency lights flashing all around the area below us, likely fire and ambulance services, as no one knew whether we would come down on wheels or the belly of the craft. Very slowly, the giant metal bird glided down, and the contact between it and the earth was imperceptible. The seatbelt light was extinguished, and there was an enormous click as four hundred buckles were released at the exact same moment. And then nothing. We sat there.

After approximately forty-five minutes, the captain came back on again. "Ladies and gentlemen, when a plane is on the ground, there are pins in the landing gear to keep it stable. Those pins, once removed, are handed to the captain, and I have them here in the cockpit with the Laker logo on them. However, there is currently a dispute between Laker Airlines and the ground crew that someone has put unmarked pins in the landing gear in an attempt to sabotage the flight. Fortunately, although the landing gear could not properly retract because of those pins, it did go down and fix itself in place. The aircraft is now being checked and refuelled, and we will be on our way as soon as everything is complete. I apologize for the inconvenience." With the end of that announcement, a wave of excited chatter swept through the compartments.

Eventually, we were off again, headed for Gatwick Airport. Our seven-hour flight took over twelve very stressful hours. Once on the ground at our planned destination, the captain thanked us for flying Laker and hoped we would fly Laker again. As if! His voice had taken on a weary, gravelly tone, almost unrecognizable from the man who had spoken to us initially.

As I required assistance, I was one of the last off the plane. As I stepped through the exit, an airport employee with a crackling radio took me into his arms and hugged me with all his might. "We have been so worried about you," he said in a warm Cockney accent. "I am so glad that you are safe."

I don't think it had occurred to any of us passengers that the staff at Gatwick knew there was a problem and that they were not just standing around waiting for a delayed flight. Indeed, they very concerned about our safety while preparing to deal with a potential disaster.

Because of the late arrival, Margaret and Eric in Kent picked me up at the airport and took me back to their home for some rest. I was already late for school, and they felt that under the circumstances, a few more hours wouldn't make any difference.

The strange thing is that I have absolutely no memory of anything from after the man hugging me until I awoke on Margaret and Eric's couch. I did not know where I was and, although they assured me that I had eaten a Spanish omelette and salad and had drunk a glass of wine, I do not remember any of it. I never liked eggs and so didn't usually eat them, and I didn't drink alcohol, so I must have been in shock to have enjoyed that meal, which they say I did.

Coincidentally or not, there had been a film on television that weekend about a plane being sabotaged by someone preventing the aircraft's landing gear from retracting properly. As I was late getting back to the school, my classmates were waiting for me. They were afraid that I had decided not to return, and when they heard about the attempted sabotage of my flight, having seen the film, they were overwhelmed with concern. I never expected the greeting I received, but I was met with great affection and assurance that I belonged there. They were all so glad that I was back!

In January of our first year of study, we were all subjected to the Progress Board. The staff sat around a boardroom table, and each student was ushered in one at a time. We were given a synopsis of how we were doing, whether we were meeting the expected standards and/or whether we had areas where we could improve. The meetings were held on a Friday, and for those students the board felt did not meet the standard and did not likely have what it would take to get up to speed with the demands of the rigorous course, it was their last day. I witnessed this for a couple of students in subsequent years, and it caused a terrible stress on everyone. Those students immediately returned to their rooms, started packing, and arranged their transportation home. This was particularly difficult for those who lived in far-flung places like South Africa or New Zealand. Students would pitch in to help pack, call an airline, or do anything else that was needed, but it was very emotional. Come Monday morning when that person was not in class, there was a bit of an emptiness in everyone. At my meeting, I was simply told that I could do better academically, which I knew; however, it was felt that I should stay in the program. What they should have said is that my test results could be higher, but my practical skills were second to none. They had no difficulty being critical but lacked positive effusiveness.

Now that I was settling in, I started participating in some of the extra-curricular activities. Much to my delight, a tandem cycling group was organized that was headquartered at the school but available to all blind people in London. It was supported by a group of volunteer sighted front riders. Philip Burton, the young man who started the group, somehow managed to acquire several tandems and triplets, which were bicycles built for three. We tended to go out cycling twice per week, once during an evening and once on the weekend. Often, it was only me who wanted to go out, and I never missed an opportunity. I usually rode on a triplet, as I liked having the third seat available for someone else. It wasn't all that much fun for three people to ride together all the time, as it could be cumbersome, but it was a great laugh to pick up hitchhikers, as it were.

One Sunday afternoon, we happened past a pub that had just been let out. One of the people standing on the pavement hollered at us for a lift. We stopped and invited him on the third seat. His friends cheered and clapped as we cycled away. We only went a few blocks, with him laughing lager fumes over me, before returning him back to his buddies. He was delighted and thanked us profusely.

On another occasion, we were riding through Hyde Park and passing Speakers' Corner when a gentleman commented on the uniqueness of the triplet bicycle. We stopped to chat to him when he told us he was a baroque musician. He played the recorder and was just passing some time before going to the airport for a flight to Germany, where he was scheduled to play in several concerts. Noticing the time, he said he would have to hurry off to get on the Tube before he was late. We offered the third seat, which he eagerly took, and with his instrument case in hand, we cycled off to the Tube station. He was the epitome of a sophisticated gentleman and likely not dressed for cycling, but he was nonetheless delighted and grateful for the unexpected experience.

Just like Christmas, the school was to be closed over Easter, and I had to find a place to go. Phil suggested that a group of us take a tandem trip to Paris. Although I had no idea what it would entail, I was quick to sign up. One of the non-teaching staff offered me accommodations for the few days before Good Friday, which was the day we set off.

Now, it is here that I must point out a very important lesson in life. If one is a student and offered a place to stay for a night or two, one should first investigate the accommodations before accepting. I was told that my generous acquaintance lived with her boyfriend in a flat. Granted, it was a flat of sorts, but much to my surprise, it was what we would call a *bachelor* in Canada. That is, there was no separate bedroom, just a large room that had a bed at one end and a table somewhere else in the open area. Initially, I was made comfortable on an air mattress with a sleeping bag. I fell asleep quite quickly, but unfortunately, was awakened near midnight. At first, I wasn't certain what had awakened me, but then I heard it—rustle, rustle, pant, pant . . . She kept saying, "Hush, you'll wake Ruth."

I kept thinking, *too late!* I held my breath for fear that they would realize I was awake and an unwilling witness. I didn't dare move. Finally, everything went quiet and, after a reasonable amount of time, I turned over and went back to sleep. However, it was enough to put me off sex for a lifetime.

Back to cycling. We only used the tandems for this trip. We were a group of nine pairs and one single cycler who came along for the fun of it.

My front rider was a young math teacher named David Wells. His mother taught French, so he was bilingual. The single cyclist was a young engineering student named Hans Roth. Hans's mother was from Switzerland, and he, too, was bilingual. We started at the school on Good Friday morning and cycled all day until we reached Brighton. It is hard to imagine now that David and I pedalled over the South Downs without getting off the bike once to walk. We were fit and certainly earned that wonderful long glide down into Brighton after the long climb up. We slept on the floors in the homes of the Brighton Cycling Club members. I happened to be staying in the home of a vegetarian. I remember it well, as I was ravenously hungry and, although not all that much of a carnivore, a plate of legumes and potatoes didn't quite cut it. Nevertheless, I slept well, and the next morning, I ate thick slices of toast and jam before setting off again.

We cycled to New Haven, where we boarded the Sealink ferry to France. There were 450 people on that boat along with cars, trucks, buses, and tandems. One could not imagine that such a large vessel with so much weight could be tossed into the English Channel like a cork. The waves were washing over the top deck, and everyone was seasick; that is, everyone but me. The Newfoundland blood in my veins came in handy. I found my way to the dining room and sat down to a meal of steak and onion pie, peas, tomatoes, and chips. The waiter was attentive, as I was the only one there. After approximately four hours, the vessel finally came to stability alongside the dock at Dieppe. It was a rather poignant arrival for me, as I was very aware that my father had landed on continental Europe at the same place about forty years earlier amid the guns of war.

It was Easter Saturday, and the town was alive with the bustle of excited Easter preparations after the long abstinence of Lent. We leaned the bikes together and left someone in charge as we went in search of food and drink. It was a beautiful day, and many of the merchants were selling their wares out on the street. One particular stall belonged to a bakery. The aroma of fresh pastry was overwhelming and, once we made our way through the crowd, we discovered croissants being sold in the great outdoors. For only twenty centimes, I was soon munching on a hot, buttery French delight. I purchased a few to share with my cycling buddies, and we went off to buy the rest of what would be our lunch. Once stuffed with French bread, cheese, and milk, we hopped back on the bikes and headed to Rouen.

No matter how cushioned or well-designed the seat of a bicycle, no one can avoid a certain amount of under-carriage or peroneal pain after being on a bike for the better part of two days. Consequently, the last thing one needs is to ride over poorly maintained cobblestone streets. Such was the situation that greeted us upon entering the city of Rouen. Fortunately, we didn't have far to ride to get to our hotel. Grenier was expensive, but they advertised each room could accommodate four people, so we took several rooms and divided up into groups. I don't know the health and safety standards of 1982 France, but in order to get to our rooms, we had to climb a steep staircase. I had just cycled for two days, so fitness was not an issue—but accessibility . . .

Out of approximately twenty steps, there were at least three risers missing, leaving gaping holes that one could fall through if one were, say, blind. I had to learn a sequence of two, jump, four, jump, and the reverse. I managed, but only thanks to a good memory and youthful agility. As we were an uneven number with the single cyclist, we had five people in our room—four young men and me. It was a little like home growing up, except that I had never shared a room, let alone a bed, with my brothers.

The next morning was Easter Sunday, and we planned for the day over a bowl of steaming coffee and French bread with thin, watery jam. Many in the group wanted to get to Paris in the quickest, most direct way. They decided to follow the railway tracks. David, Hans, and I were in not such a hurry to get to our destination, as we also wanted to enjoy the journey. We decided to leave the group and ride along the Seine. It would undoubtedly take us longer to arrive in Paris, but we felt it preferable.

A continental breakfast is not the sort of sustenance one requires to cycle over one hundred kilometres in one day. We agreed that at the first opportunity for food, we would stop. Before long, we came upon a café and went in for nourishment. We were informed that as it was a café, they did not serve food. However, farther into the village, we might find a shop open. So we ordered coffee and pulled out our map to see where we were and where we had to go. The other patrons left their tables and excitedly surrounded us with questions about who we were and what we were doing.

Tandem bikes always draw attention, and this was no exception. The men grabbed our map and debated over the best way to go. They finally came to a consensus and all stood outside, cheering and waving us on. *"Bonne chance!"*

Once in the middle of the village, we came upon a millstream that flowed gently under a little bridge. I sat on the bank of the stream with the bikes and waited for the boys to hopefully return with food. David and Hans did return with lunch and spread out a picnic like no other. They found a market that had been about to close, and they'd bought a baguette, foie gras, camembert cheese, yogurt, dark chocolate, and milk. It was a beautiful, sunny Easter Sunday, and we sat there by the millstream and sang, "How Great Thou Art."

Following along the Seine provided us a wonderful microcosm view of French life. We passed industrial factories and warehouses, quiet that Sunday. There were lovely farms with cows and sheep as well as fine gentry homes with locals enjoying the day on horseback. As late afternoon turned into evening, we came to a place where we had to cross over the river. It was in a small town that conveniently had a pub. We went in but received an awkward, frosty greeting. Undaunted, we sat at a table and pulled out the map and waited to be served. After a brief moment, one of my companions realized that there were only men there, and hence the cool reception at the sight of me. My buddies explained to the waiter who we were and what we were doing, and the atmosphere thawed slightly. Perhaps they thought better of throwing a blind woman out onto the street. The boys ordered beer, and I ordered a lemonade, but when we asked to see a menu, we were informed that, as it was Easter Sunday, they were not serving food and could not help us. When the waiter returned with our drinks, he asked where we were from.

In my best French, I said, *"Je suis Canadienne."*

The atmosphere warmed significantly. Did I have any Canadian money, postcards, or souvenirs? Apparently, the man serving us was the pub owner and liked to collect keepsakes from foreign travellers. Unfortunately, I disappointed him, but the atmosphere remained warm. After sitting there and nursing our beverages for about half an hour and worrying about where we might get some food, the waiter returned to our table with three giant ham and cheese baguette sandwiches. Surprised but delighted, we tried to pay for them while casually commenting that we thought they had no food. Gesturing to a man across the pub, he said, "Pierre went home, and his wife made them for you." Simple kindness, a true blessing.

Once over the bridge and cycling down the other side of the Seine, we headed straight for Paris. It was about eight that evening when David informed me we had just entered the City of Lights. Before long, David said, "Ruth, we are passing the Arc de Triomphe, and it is just as well you are blind because the traffic is scary."

We stayed at the Fédération des Aveugles, a hostel for blind people, where we received kindness. On Easter Monday, we toured Paris. I was taken into Notre-Dame by David Norman, a PhD chemistry student and someone else's front rider. Again, it was a beautiful day. As we walked by the area of sacred artifacts, there was an ear-splitting rumble.

"Thunder, on a day like today?"

"No," said David, "a bomb!"

"Bomb? Are you sure?" I quivered.

"Yes, Ruth. I am a chemist, and believe me, I know what a chemical explosion looks like." David gently said, "Ruth, we are going to be calm. We will walk slowly toward the door, and we will not panic."

Fortunately, there was not much to burn in the cathedral as it was mainly stone, but that didn't stop a huge group of American tourists from rushing past us and going in the other direction to take pictures of whatever flame and damage there was. Moving calmly, David informed me that I would soon feel the fresh air of the outdoors as we were close to an exit. I have never felt such relief as I did when the cool breeze brushed me and welcomed me outside.

The next morning, I awoke with a fever. When I did not show up for breakfast, the woman who ran the hostel came storming into my room to toss me out of bed. There were very strict rules in that place, and I had apparently broken a big one by not getting up and out by a certain hour. Upon discovering me in an undeniably sickly state, she felt compassion, returned to her office, and made a phone call to someone, presumably a doctor or pharmacist, who then provided me with medicine that helped immensely. Once I had improved, we rode the bikes to the train station and boarded a train back to London.

For some reason, our principal, David Teager, did not like the tandem club being run out of the school, or perhaps he just didn't like Phil, the chap who ran it, but Phil was a go-getter and took every opportunity to profile the club and garner support. On the one hand, here was a young man who wanted to facilitate blind people having the same opportunities as sighted people. This was especially true for cycling, including recreational cycling, tourism cycling, and marathon racing. On the other hand, we had a principal who was widely involved in the world of physiotherapy to an international level and, although likely proud of the school's blind and visually impaired physiotherapists, he didn't want us to appear blind. We were not allowed to use a white cane on the wards of the hospitals, which is outrageous when one considers the number of obstacles and therefore potential dangers to us and the patients. The explanation for this and other restrictions was to aid in the comfort of the patients and their acceptance of us; however, one must wonder whose acceptance of us was truly in doubt. Hence the almost impossible spatial awareness test to gain entry into the school. Consequently, one can understand the inevitable collision between a man who accepts disability and wants to enhance life and another man who hopes to find and exploit the super blind for some sort of self-aggrandizement. We were not to appear blind, and it might even have been preferable if we were not blind at all. Hence the small ratio of blind to visually impaired students at the school, four out of forty-four and perhaps the lack of orientation on admission.

On June 5, 1982, there was an Adventure Day at Battersea Park in South London. I believe it was a day to promote activity and fitness, and there were many groups, clubs, and organizations scheduled to be profiled there. Our tandem club was just such a group. It was rumoured that Prince Charles would be attending the event and might even speak to some of the participants. As Prince Charles was the patron of our cycling club, it was hoped that he might make us one of his stops.

There were a lot of people milling about, looking at our bikes and asking questions when, suddenly, a Rolls-Royce and a whole gaggle of photographers stopped at our display. Out of the car stepped Prince Charles. He asked a few standard questions and talked about "the great fun he had at Cambridge on a bicycle built for six."

When asked if he would like a ride on a triplet, he said yes, but inquired what to do with the legs of his trousers. Someone suggested that he tuck his royal trousers into his royal socks. I don't know what he did. I only know that as he mounted the second seat where I usually sat, a flurry of people fought to get on the third seat. As I was the most avid and consistent cyclist in the club, Phil, who was about six foot four or more, picked me up and dropped me onto the last seat. One of our regular front riders, Bruce, was on the first seat, and away we went. The photographers tried to run after us and take pictures, but we kicked it into high gear and left them running back to get into their vehicles to try and catch up.

A tandem or triplet is constructed so that the handlebars of the second or third seat are fitted under the seat of the rider ahead. Consequently, by grasping the handlebars, it appeared that my hands were sort of tucked under the Prince's bottom.

Quietly, he said to me, "Don't touch the bum."

Slightly offended, I assured him that I was not interested in "the bum."

After that, we just carried on happily, free from care and the paparazzi. We covered about two kilometres when we hit a rough patch. "Christ, that's the end of a happily married existence," whined the Prince. Although we have been led to believe otherwise, I think it was a pretty exciting time in his life, as Prince William was born within the next two weeks. The next morning, the newspapers were full of the Battersea Park events and Prince Charles's participation. The best headline came from *The Mirror*: "The Pedalling Prince of Wheels."

Phil talked about organizing a yearlong cycling trip across Europe. I expressed interest as long as it occurred after I qualified as a physiotherapist. It was a big dream, as it would be difficult, although not necessarily impossible, to get permission to ride through the Iron Curtain countries. However, Phil was up to trying. Sadly, the dream disappeared along with any future cycling adventures when someone broke into the school garage and stole all the bikes. Both sides of the colliding factions pointed fingers at each other, but it didn't matter to me who was responsible. I was just heartbroken.

CHAPTER 11

I have always been afraid of fire, or at least since a very young age. When I was eight, I was home for the weekend from school in Brantford. It was a Friday evening, and Peach, her friend Grace, and I were at the church preparing the altar for Sunday. They had put on the kettle to make a cup of tea when I said that I heard crackling.

"That is just the kettle," Peach assured me.

"No, Mommy, I hear the kettle, but there is another crackling noise over there."

Turning to see where I was gesturing, Peach was horrified to see the back of the church ablaze with flames licking up the windows. She sent me to the front door to go outside, which I did, but the front door had a sticky lock, and that brief moment of fiddling with the lock struck panicked fear in my heart. Nevertheless, the door did eventually open, and I ran onto the front lawn, shaking in terror. Peach snatched down the massive, heavy fire extinguisher and headed around the back of the building. There was a man standing there, likely the arsonist, and she thrust the extinguisher into his hands and instructed him to put out the flames. He sprinkled a little at the inferno, dropped the equipment, and left. Peach grabbed up the extinguisher and fought the fire until she won the battle. By the time the fire brigade arrived, it was over.

Unfortunately, I was a sleepwalker, and after that, my problem increased. I could do almost anything in my sleep and because of it, Peach feared that I would open the door and walk outside. As a result, she put a lock on the front door that was beyond my reach. Eventually, the sleepwalking stopped, but the fear of fire did not.

Early one January morning of my first year in physiotherapy school, I was partially brought to a conscious state by a ringing noise outside my door, and then I was abruptly fully awakened as one of my unit mates banged on my door yelling, "Fire!" I had spoken of my fear, and so one of the other students ensured I heard the alarm. It was a false alarm, but we all stood outside and talked about what we would save if it were an actual fire. One fellow stated he would grab his stereo, while others named treasures they would not like to lose.

One of our lecturers, Sue Bentley-Beard, was also the deputy residence manager. She lived in a suite in the school, but we rarely saw her outside of class unless we needed something on a weekend when she was in charge. Sue was a very fine teacher and very bright woman, but unfortunately, she had a hearing deficit. Later that day as we were all discussing the false alarm in class, she clearly knew nothing about it. She had not heard the alarm while sleeping. With a pensive sadness in her voice, she said, "No one came to save me." My heart sank, and I wept for her inside.

Not long after that, on a Friday evening, I returned to my room after dinner to work on an essay. Many of the students who had not gone home for the weekend were out on dates or at the pub. As I kept the Sabbath holy and therefore did no studying or work on Sundays, I had to study on Friday evening and Saturday. It was my custom to always remove my shoes and put on my slippers as soon as I entered my room, but for some unknown reason, that evening, I thought I wouldn't bother taking off my shoes and instead go directly to my desk and start writing. Within an hour of working on my essay, the fire alarm went off again. Recalling the previous incident, I thought, Now, if this were a real fire, what would I save?

Leaping to my feet, I said out loud, "Myself!" and ran for the door. As soon as I headed for the stairs, I smelled the acrid smoke. Running down one flight, I heard those sad words ringing in my heart: No one came to save me.

The manager saw me and yelled, "Where do you think you're going?"

"I am going to get Sue," I yelled back over the ear-splitting ring of the alarm.

"Ruth, she knows! Get out! It is real!"

Heading back to the stairway, just outside where the fire was burning, I came upon Pat, a newly blind Irish girl who was bewildered by the constant ringing and was running in circles yelling, "Help me, I don't know where I am!"

Rushing to her I yelled, "Pat, it's Ruth." I grabbed her arm, and we ran furiously toward the stairs and down. We went so fast that, although we were the last to leave, we were some of the first out. We passed people on the stairs, clinging to the railing with the alarm deafening us and the smoke burning our eyes. Finally, we went through the emergency exit into the great outdoors. Typical of London, it was raining. Was I ever glad to be wearing my shoes!

As the whole incident was playing out, I had no fear, and my thoughts were clear, but once I was back in my room, I became jelly. My heart was pounding and my legs like rubber, but as I sat reflecting, I eventually realized that I could manage in an emergency, and it went a long way to help me with my fear, which is now improved but not gone.

The fire had been caused by a visually impaired person who felt it was okay to put a lid on a pot of oil to get it hot enough to deep-fry some sort of South African doughnut-like concoction. The oil became hot, all right. It burned through a fire blanket and melted the taps in the sink after she threw the pot there and poured water on it. She didn't make it as a physiotherapist either.

No one came to speak to us over the weekend to review what had happened, nor were we ever offered any counselling. However, on Monday morning, I was called to Principal Teager's office. I was asked by him what had happened on Friday. Apparently, he was only interested in the part where I was found dashing across the building to Sue's suite. I explained that I wanted to ensure she got out safely. Well, let it be said that Principal Teager was not pleased with me, telling me, "Our insurance does not cover heroes."

Oh, this was not about people; it was about money! I felt as though I was being chastised for caring. The chartered Society of Physiotherapy pin, which qualified therapists wear proudly, displays, among other things, two hands holding to symbolize the caring profession. Why did they think I had applied for the course? Did they expect any less caring from someone who wanted to be a pin-wearing member of the caring profession? I was forced to agree that, if it happened again, I would simply run out, but in my heart, I knew that if it ever did happen again, I would help anyone who needed me! I would rather be a dead hero than live with someone's demise on my conscience when I could have done something about it.

As the first year drew to a close, we were subjected to the "part one" national physiotherapy exams. This included written papers and an oral anatomy test. I was becoming one of the better anatomy and biomechanics students, and there was great hope for me. However, I have always had examination nerves, and the part ones were no exception. I presented myself at the Regional Examination Centre at the Prince of Wales School of Physiotherapy, where my anatomy viva was to take place. I was introduced to the model I would be using for demonstration purposes, a physio student from somewhere else, and so began the twenty-minute firing squad of questions.

I froze in fear. I stood there and said little to nothing. The questions were unbelievably easy: Show me the radial pulse. Demonstrate the movements of the glenohumeral joint, etc. I knew it all but was silent. There is some sort of rule of nature in education that one can know it all, but if one does not answer the questions, one will fail!

And I did. I was home for the summer vacation when I received the phone call from Principal Teager. "Miss Vallis, you have been unsuccessful in completing the part one examinations." His words were brief and cold. I suppose one can't expect warm and fuzzy at a time like that.

I asked what I could do about it, and he told me I could apply to try again. The call ended abruptly, but then, it was long distance and, of course, money came before people. I fought tears, more from embarrassment than anything else. I believed that I would have had what it took to pass if I could conquer my nerves.

I returned to the school in September, where I attended the opening assembly. The vice-principal smacked me on the back and growled, "What happened to you?" I know that they were disappointed, as they'd had high hopes for me, but no higher than what I'd had for myself. I was treated like a pariah. I revised day and night while still attending classes and writing and submitting the assignments required for the second-year course. All the while, staff spoke to me as little as possible and quietly made snide comments like, "Why bother?" I was not the only student who failed, but seemingly, I was the biggest disappointment.

Finally, in October, the day for the re-examination arrived, and off I went again. Trying to keep my nerves in check, I started a little shakily by referring to the examiner as "Sir" before realizing that the gruff, rather deep voice belonged to a woman. I quickly corrected myself and, after no reaction from her, I proceeded to answer the barrage of questions. However, this time, they were not nearly so simple. Thanking my examiner and model, I left mumbling about nailing the lid on my physiotherapy casket while wondering what my second career choice might be. Thankfully, much to the delight of everyone, I passed, and I quickly turned my undivided attention to fully catching up on my second-year work.

While at home on vacation between my first and second year, I met Clive Reddin. I was good friends with a very popular radio announcer, Bill Robinson. Bill used to arrange social events for his listeners. He invited me to join him at one of them and go out for dinner afterwards, just the two of us. I met Clive at that event, and he asked for my phone number. Many people met at those events, and Bill, who was twenty years my senior, was pleased for me. By the end of that summer, Clive and I became engaged to be married. Coincidentally, he and his family were from England, living in Canada, while I was from Canada, living in England. Clive was a gentle chap with a corny sense of humour. He was a voracious reader and would eagerly read out loud to me on any topic. He loved and had a great knowledge of history, especially military battles. He served as a volunteer in the Canadian Reserves while working in a printing company as he awaited acceptance into the Canadian Armed Forces as a full-time soldier. We discussed at great length what the challenges would be for me if the military moved us around Canada and, indeed, the world, but he always felt confident and spoke reassuringly of our ability to manage together.

My parents liked Clive and supported the wedding plans, as he made a concerted effort to establish himself in my life and circle of friends. He attended my church, although I was not there, and participated in activities to get to know everyone. Marilyn's father took one of those occasions to ask Clive if he was certain about marrying me. Mr. Colhoun suggested that being married to a blind person could be very difficult and that Clive should reconsider. Upon hearing about this unsolicited advice, my parents were livid at his audacity. Fearing that I would hear about the conversation, Clive relayed it to me with the same reassuring words with which he had replied to Mr. Colhoun. Referring to Eleanor Roosevelt's statement about her husband years earlier, Clive said, "If Eleanor can be Franklin's legs, I can be Ruth's eyes."

Unfortunately, immersion into an intensive course of study does not need to be, neither should it be, encumbered by a long-distance relationship, especially with the added burden of long-term commitment plans. Distance has a way of distorting perspective.

As I mentioned, with every decision we make in life, there will be change, and we have to live with the consequences. Whether we are choosing to get married, have a child, take on a mortgage, move locations, select a career or accept a job, things will never be the same as they were—which is not to suggest that they may not be better. Therefore, before taking any plunge, we must weigh all the components of our decision and be clear and honest with ourselves about those things we are not prepared to compromise and those things that we would be willing to sacrifice. The question we must ask ourselves is, *is this going to make my life better, or is it going to make my life worse?*

I had no idea whether I would be successful and qualify as a physiotherapist and, if so, where I would work. This in itself would be a life-changing event. The man who'd asked me to marry him was asking a student, and that was different than marrying a qualified professional. In the time since the proposal, we had been evolving into different people, and the distance was preventing us from evolving together. Our conversations were very lopsided with him just plodding along while my days were filled with new challenges, new people, and new ideas. I asked him to take a few days off work and fly to London so I could introduce him to some favourite places and people; at the same time, we would be able to talk things over together and, hopefully, relieve some of the stress that was building. However, he declined, as he felt the money for the flight would be better put toward our future.

I awoke one night and thought, *It will not be long now, and I will not be waking up alone.* Suddenly, my stomach turned over. I was surprised by the feeling, so I repeated the statement. *It will not be long now, and I will not be waking up alone.* Wham! I felt sick. It was wrong. It was all wrong. I couldn't marry him, but I had to marry him. I had made a promise, and I was a person of integrity. I felt sick, and my mind spun out of control.

I decided to end the engagement. There were too many pieces in a complex picture that was nowhere near complete, so the decision was the prudent one—perhaps being more of God's interventional wisdom than my own.

I flew home for Easter, as I did not want to tell Clive over the phone, but at the same time, it could not wait. As soon as we arrived at my parents' house from the airport, my folks made themselves scarce so Clive and I could get reacquainted, not knowing what was about to happen. I removed my engagement ring, pressed it into the palm of Clive's hand and said, "I can't marry you." Immediately, I had an overwhelming sense of relief, as though the greatest albatross had been lifted from my shoulders.

Sadly for Clive, I was so relieved that I was completely unmoved by his tearful statement: "I knew it was too good to be true."

I returned to school happily after the vacation, unencumbered by the added stress of the long-distance relationship demands. Several months later, while walking around London with Marilyn's friend Barbara Cherry, she suddenly said, "Thank you, Ruth, on behalf of women everywhere, for leaving Clive behind to answer the awkward questions about what happened."

When I had entered my second year, I had determined that new students coming into the school would not struggle as I had done. I offered information about the school and physiotherapy program as well as orientation to the community. Other students also assisted to make the transition smoother.

Now that the tandems were gone, I needed a new sporting outlet. We were offered golfing lessons. A few of us took the opportunity and went on Monday evenings to a local school gymnasium for instruction. My two good friends, Michelle Jackson and Joanne Beavers, a couple of Yorkshire lassies, also became regular students of the game. Once spring arrived and the weather improved, we took our lessons outdoors on Friday evenings at the Three Rivers sports stadium, where we went from simply driving to chipping and putting. We would stop at the local fish and chip shop on the way home and, all in all, it was a great way to de-stress at the end of the week.

Although Peach sent me a small care package every three weeks and I received an occasional letter from Marilyn, without email or cellphones, communication across the Atlantic was difficult. If I wanted to make a long-distance call home, I had to arrange it with the women in the school office. This meant a very narrow window of opportunity, given the five-hour time difference and the limited office hours.

A curious thing happened one Sunday. I awoke feeling compelled to call Marilyn. The only way I could do it on a Sunday was to go farther into town to the international pay phones. A good friend and fellow student with reasonable mobility vision, Dewi Perkins, agreed to accompany me after church. I gathered the required fifty pence pieces and waited in the long line for my turn. I didn't know why I felt the way I did, only that I had to speak with Marilyn immediately.

Once at the front of the line, I pushed a coin into the slot and, just as I was about to dial, the coin popped out again. I repeated the process a couple of times with the same result. Thinking the coin might be somehow faulty, I tried another coin, but it happened again. Dewi and I agreed that there had been quite a queue ahead of us, so perhaps the coin receptacle was full. As we stepped aside, the person behind me inserted a coin and made his call. Discouraged, we walked away, agreeing that the best thing would be for me to call from the office tomorrow, Monday.

For some reason, that feeling of urgent need to call Marilyn was not there on Monday. In fact, I had forgotten my plan, but Tuesday was a different story. I awoke once again with the same overwhelming feeling that I must call Marilyn right away. I arranged with the office administrators to call at lunch so I would get her before she left for school. When she answered the phone, I told her about my feeling on Sunday and the problems I'd had with the phone.

"I am okay, Ruth," she said. "Everything went well." I had no idea what she was talking about. Then she explained that doctors had found a large mass in her abdomen. She'd gone to the hospital on Monday, the day before, for surgery. Naturally, everyone at church was praying for her but, more surprisingly, the children in her class gad requested and received permission to offer a public prayer for her during morning messages as well. Once on the operating table, the surgeon could no longer find the growth, and she was sent home. "Ruth, I have received a miracle, and you don't have to worry anymore." I had been worried, although I hadn't known why, but I think I received a miracle, too.

Fortunately, there were no national examinations at the end of second year. I was completing all my written assignments, numerous practical exams, and clinical placements that were my strength and pleasure. However, I knew my third year would be the real challenge. First of all, we spent much more time in clinical placements, and some of the hospitals were so far afield that I would have to stay in residence from Sunday to Friday and only return to the school for weekends. There would be the selection and completion of a final major project and the final part, two national exams that would cover all topics studied from the first day of the three-year program.

CHAPTER 12

The difficulty with post-secondary study is finding the fine balance between giving the lecturers and clinical tutors/supervisors what one thinks they want and, at the same time, trying to maintain a piece of oneself. Although there is a side to Britain that is progressive and accepting, there is the other side that hasn't changed in a thousand years.

The latter is the side with the great expectations of decorum and professionalism, especially in careers such as physiotherapy that have always been considered middle class. While I handled myself professionally, some situations demanded a more casual interaction, and I feared that this approach could be considered unprofessional. Fortunately, there are those defining moments in one's life where the *aha!* light bulb goes off in one's head and we gather the required confidence to be ourselves. There were three incidences that occurred during my third year that were likely the most influential factors in my transition from student physiotherapist into the clinician I became.

I have always had a soft spot for elderly people. Perhaps it stems from growing up in a church where there were always plenty of older folk with capabilities, gifts, and talents that I admired from my earliest days. Consequently, I was delighted at the end of my second year to have a clinical placement in a geriatric day hospital at Barnet General in North London. In fact, I ended up having two such placements, the second being an elective at the insistence of the patients. The program was mainly for elderly people, living in the community but failing to thrive. They were brought in daily for several sessions involving their assessment and treatment by a team of clinicians. After lunch, they would all sit in big armchairs with footstools and have a rest before doing some chair exercises and then continuing with their individual afternoon sessions.

When it was discovered that I played the guitar, I was encouraged to bring it in, and we sang while doing the chair class. However, I refused to sing naughty songs no matter how much some of the old ladies begged me, but it was mainly because I didn't know any. One insisted that she be allowed to teach me "Knees Up Mother Brown," but I insisted that I was a lady, and she reluctantly relented.

On my last day, those so-called failing-to-thrive older people managed to organize a party for me, which included some of them bringing in cake, other snacks, and beverages. It was a wonderful learning experience, but there was one particular patient I shall never forget: George Wilson. I mention his name because I never want him to be forgotten.

George was a man in his sixties with a rather rare condition called syringomyelia. He was unable to perceive pain. Now, one might say, "How fortunate!" but it was not so. If he placed his hand on a hot stove, he could be badly burned without knowing it. He could get appendicitis and he would not be warned by pain if his appendix burst. He'd had it all his life and, in his youth, it had been treated very primitively, which left him with huge problems. He was in a wheelchair and unable to lift or hold up his own head. His cheek was perpetually on his chest. However, he was very bright and had been a medical journal proofreader. He had no family and had been relegated to living in a residence for the elderly since he'd been about fifty. Not having much in common with the elderly people, he'd also ended up with no friends. I was assigned to treat him. As I worked with him on rolling from side to side in bed to improve his independence with transferring from his bed to his wheelchair, we chatted about everything. We both looked forward to the days he was scheduled to be there. He was sorry to see me go, but I hoped that I had made some difference in his life over the few short weeks we worked together in June.

Come the September of my third year, my first placement was for six weeks in burns and plastics at Mount Vernon Hospital in Northwood. We regularly did breakfast rounds, which meant the whole care team would march from patient to patient, starting about seven in the morning. In that land where some things never change, the consultant physician, chief doctor, or surgeon would lead the team that followed in a hierarchical parade with students bringing up the rear. The fear of most in the group was that the consultant would turn, point at someone, and ask a difficult question. Of course, this was for the purpose of education, but it often resulted in more embarrassment than learning.

One morning as we were proceeding through the ward, we came to a patient that I had not yet met, so I just leaned against the wall while those who knew him talked to him. The team was large, and I hoped to be inconspicuous at the back, well away from the consultant's view and, therefore, from questions.

Suddenly the patient asked, "Is that my Ruth?"

Uncertain of what he meant, the surgeon turned to see to whom he was referring. "Are you Ruth?" the consultant asked me.

I needed prompting from the others that he was talking to me. I said I was.

"This gentleman seems to know you and would like to speak with you."

As I moved toward the bed, the surgeon urged everyone else away and, with compassion in his voice, suggested that I be left alone with the patient.

"Ruth, it's George Wilson," he whispered, unable to do much more.

I inquired what he was doing in this hospital. He told me he was very sick. There was something wrong with his stomach, cancer, I learned later, and this was the best centre to address his needs. I spoke with him for a while and visited him a couple of times, but then, once again, the placement was over, and I moved on to another hospital.

Just before Christmas, I was back in class after twelve weeks in placement when I was called to the vice-principal's office. "We have a message for you from Mount Vernon Hospital."

I hadn't been there in almost two months, so was surprised that anyone there would be contacting me. "Ruth, George Wilson has died."

Although glad to be informed, I asked why they thought to call me.

"Because, Ruth, you are down as his next of kin. He had no one else."

I inquired about a funeral, but he had already been placed somewhere in England in a pauper's grave. Oh, my aching heart.

During a general medical placement, my supervisor introduced me to a gentleman she was treating, or, perhaps I should say, trying to treat. He had suffered a very dense stroke that left him without any use of his entire right side and speech. Evidently very discouraged, he would not respond to any instructions or make any attempt to communicate in any way. My supervisor was a very experienced clinician, possibly close to retirement. I am not certain whether she introduced me to that patient for my own interest and learning or whether she was hoping I would have a suggestion on how to reach him. Out of simple curiosity, I asked her to tell me about him. She seemed to know very little (which is never a good thing) except that he had been a church organist. Although I was close to the end of my training, I still feared saying or doing the wrong thing, especially with those who were marking my performance. Be that as it may, I have always been a great lover of traditional church hymns and had several tape recordings of instrumental and choir renditions of dozens of well-known pieces.

As part of my orientation for that particular placement, I was shown a locked room that was a quiet place for the express purpose of physio-therapy treatments for those patients who might require or do better in a quiet one-on-one treatment. I don't think that room was often used, as it took some setting up and organization to get a patient there. However, the next morning, I asked my supervisor if she felt there was any merit in taking that gentleman to the quiet room. Perhaps getting him off the ward into a change of scenery might stimulate him a little. She acknowledged that she liked the fact that I had been thinking about it and had a plan, but she didn't know how much of a plan. She instructed me to get the room ready, and she would bring the man to me.

Initially, being in the room appeared to make no difference, but then I plucked up my courage and, with my heart in my mouth, I asked if I could try something a little different.

"Go ahead," she said, as she obviously had no other ideas and was feeling a little frustrated at her inability to reach him.

I went to a table where I had placed a little tape recorder. I switched it on. Softly, a choir began to sing, "All Creatures of our God and King." I don't remember the whole playlist, but I hummed along as I gently stretched his flexed right-upper extremity.

Gradually, he acknowledged me; the key of communication had been turned.

While receiving my final evaluation for that placement, my supervisor explained that there were many physiotherapy students who could quote chapters, pages, and paragraphs of any textbook, but that patients were not textbooks. "Ruth, I suspect you are not the best in your class at quoting from what you have read when writing an exam."

"No," I laughed.

"No, Ruth, but you are the best at reaching people. We don't treat textbooks, we treat people, and you must continue to have the courage to do the little things, like playing hymns for an organist, to ensure you reach your patients. That is an important aspect of physiotherapy, and you are a gifted physiotherapist."

The funny thing about life is that just when one feels that one has grasped things and is ready to go out and conquer the world, one is brought up short with a taste of reality. That is exactly what happened to me during the very next placement. Our school provided two women who were our clinical tutors, Mary Begg and Mary Winter. They both did some class teaching, but their main responsibility was to come and see us while we were in placement to check and see how we were managing and to also be a support to our supervising therapists—our supervisors were not usually blind or visually impaired, and may needed some help with some aspect of instruction. Mary Winter looked after us for out-patients, while Mary Begg looked after us for in-patients. We were never told ahead of time when one was coming unless there was a huge issue or we had requested a visit; Miss Begg would just appear. Due to all the students being blind or visually impaired, most of the time, she would be there watching us, and we were none the wiser.

Mary Begg had a great propensity for showing up at exactly the wrong moment. On one such occasion, a blind chap in the year ahead of me was late back from lunch and didn't know that Miss Begg was already there. She gave him a minute and then announced her presence and asked him how things were going with the treatment. Not wanting to admit his tardiness, he said that he and the patient were getting along fine and things were going very well. Unfortunately, he had not had time to figure out that there was no patient in the bed. Surprise!

I was treating a woman with pneumonia who was also totally blind and deaf. I tried to learn some simple finger spelling so I could communicate with her, but she was too ill and stressed. Her lungs required suction, which, for any patient, is a difficult procedure; but it is even worse for someone with whom we could not communicate. I was very thin in those days and was sent to stand in a narrow space between the wall and the bed. My supervising therapist stood on the other side. I was handed a catheter and instructed to suction her. Feeling overwhelming compassion, I squeezed her shoulder, stroked her cheek and attempted to pass the catheter. She clenched her teeth and shook her head violently back and forth. My supervisor and a nurse struggled to hold her head still so I could enter her nose with the tube, and I was almost finished the procedure when one of them said, "Oh, you will have to stop. There is blood in the catheter." Her thrashing about had caused the catheter to traumatize her tissues. I felt sick!

The world became very hazy, voices were moving away into the distance, my knees were buckling, and I was sliding slowly down the wall. Just before I went under the bed, Miss Begg—oh yes, apparently, she was watching—reached over and threw an arm around my waist. Dragging me out from between the bed and the wall, she whisked me out of the room and across the corridor with my feet barely touching the floor.

With one determined movement, she threw open a window, thrust my head out, and all in one breath, she snapped, "Take a big breath, pull yourself together, remember you're a professional, get back in there, and finish the job!"

I gasped for air and, barely able to stand or talk, I whispered, "Yes, ma'am," and stumbled back into the room where my supervisor said it was okay; she had finished the treatment, and I could leave.

One of the rules at the school was that the lecturers were not permitted in the residence. So I escaped the hospital, returned to my room, spoke to no one, locked my door, lay on my bed, and sobbed. About seven that evening, I was still crying into my pillow when there was a knock on my door. I made no attempt to get up or answer it.

"Ruth, it's Mary Begg. Please let me in. I would like to talk to you."

"No," I sobbed, "you're not allowed in here. Go away."

Softly, gently, she insisted.

I got up, unlocked the door, and fell back onto my bed. Miss Begg entered and took a seat across from me. She said nothing for a long while. Like Peach, she just let me get it out of my system. I spoke first. Turning toward her, I half yelled and half sobbed, "I don't want to be a physiotherapist. Physios torture people, and I don't want to be a torturer!"

After I resumed my prone face in the pillow position, she gently urged me to sit up and talk to her. "Ruth, you have a great capacity to love, but you must temper your love with professionalism. Sometimes," she went on, "we are called to do difficult things, and in this case, you were saving her life. Ruth, don't give up on physiotherapy, and don't ever stop loving."

What I felt and still feel about these three early defining moments of patient interactions were best summed up years later in a sermon delivered by a United Church of Canada minister, the late Sylvia Hamilton. She preached on the scripture Exodus 3:5, where Moses is at the burning bush, and it says, "Take off your sandals, because you are standing on Holy ground." Sylvia suggested that people, purely as a creation of God, are sacred and, therefore, in our interactions with all people, whether pauper or prince, we must recognize that we are standing on holy ground. Sylvia captured the essence of compassion, to see each person with the eyes of Christ.

If, as health care professionals, we are willing to admit that we are, by the nature of our work, perpetually standing on the holy ground of the human spirit, then we must remove the sandals of racism, ageism, sexism, disability, economics, or whatever form of prejudice may be causing a barrier to allowing us to love and extend compassion to each and every one equally. Even the Psalmist David, I believe, was pleading a similar request in Psalm 143:10, where he says, "Teach me to do your will, for you are my God; May your good spirit lead me on level ground."

Currently in healthcare, there is an increasing tendency to refer to patients as clients. I have found myself in many debates over which is the most appropriate term. My argument is that there are terms or titles that are not interchangeable, as to do so diminishes the essence of the true meaning.

There are those who would suggest that client is the appropriate term, as it refers to the provision of a service. Some argue that as patients become better informed and take greater control of their health and health care, the clinician is also changing to reflect more of an educator/facilitator role. I, however, feel that the term client is the thin edge of the sandal wedge.

Parents have children. Teachers have students. Married folk have spouses. And health care professionals have patients. Bankers, lawyers, and salespeople have clients and, although I do not deny they do important work, it is fundamentally different. While undergoing a root canal, my dentist's assistant held my hand and spoke softly during a particularly difficult moment, but if my accountant or the fellow selling me a new sofa held my hand, I would be a little suspicious and a whole lot uncomfortable. It would be foolish to deny the relevance of touch in healing. Yes, we touch our patients intellectually through education and facilitation, but we also touch them emotionally through encouragement and support and touch them physically to provide treatment and bring about comfort. Indeed, health care offers a service, but it is a service to those who are sick, injured, in pain, fearful, discouraged, lonely, and vulnerable. We must never forget that they are not bits of technology. They are now and have always been the creation of God, and we are His privileged instruments of healing. The relationship between a clinician and patient is unique and special.

CHAPTER 13

Because of the way in which professionals are trained in the UK, they run something called mock exams. This is where the students sit an entire exam, using questions from previous years, to establish one's readiness to sit the finals and to recognize any weaknesses in one's knowledge so that holes can be plugged and weaknesses strengthened before it is too late. Trying to guess what might be on the actual exam is almost a sport. With the extensive amount of material one is required to learn—the final exams cover all the material learned from the first day in year one onward—one tries to hedge one's bets by postulating what questions have never been asked and, therefore, what is likely to come up this time. In 1984, the big new trend was therapeutic ultrasound; however, hydrotherapy had been used in physiotherapy for decades, if not centuries, but had never been on the exam. I had a mental block about the physics of ultrasound and hoped that it would not be a question. On the other hand, I loved treating patients in water and had a natural understanding of the physical principles.

One of my classmates, John, had a thorough understanding of ultrasound, so I asked him if he could explain it to me. I had taught John to play the guitar and thought us on a fairly friendly footing, and so was shocked when he answered, "It is for me to know and you to find out."

I initially laughed, hoping he was joking, but fought tears when he only repeated it and walked away. I followed him, protesting that we were in this together. Once we qualified, we wouldn't be fighting for jobs in the same market, as he would go back to Ireland, and I would go home to Canada. "Is there any more glory if you pass and I fail?" I asked.

"Perhaps there is," he answered.

I returned to my room, saddened and disappointed, and spent some time in prayer asking the Lord to soften my heart about John and give me some clarity of thought about ultrasound.

The mock exams went reasonably well, but I knew what I had to do to prepare for May and June when I would be faced with the true test of my potential to be a physiotherapist. As the semester ended, we had a two-week Easter break, and I needed somewhere to go. Home was not an option for many reasons, the main one being that I needed to focus on studying without distractions. By that time, Mary Winter, my personal tutor, had left the school. Her husband had retired from his teaching position, and they returned to the family home in the Lake District of northern England. Mrs. Winter invited me to spend the Easter fortnight at their home. "Bring some books, as there will be plenty of time for quiet study," she urged.

When other students found out where I would be for the holiday, they responded with gossip and snide comments about favouritism. I even heard some of the teaching staff voice disapproval, but as they offered no alternatives, I put it down to jealousy and tried to dismiss it.

Mrs. Winter's middle son, Ted, met me off the train in Carlisle. Ted was a fine young Christian man home on vacation from Manchester University. We were greeted at the house by Gran, Mrs. Winter's mother, who had a beautiful dinner of Turkish lamb prepared for us. Mr. and Mrs. Winter were away in Greece and would not be home for several days, leaving Ted and I relegated to the doting care of a sweet grandmother.

The winter home was three old cottages converted into one lovely house with a beautiful, sunny living room, perfect for reading the morning papers, petting the big old cat, and enjoying coffee and biscuits at eleven. At the back, there was a small hothouse with lots of vegetables, a prolific plum tree, and a rose garden. Oh yes, and beyond that, there was a sort of meadow in which resided a pony. Idyllic.

They were still receiving milk in bottles on the doorstep. My breakfast would begin with honey nut cornflakes bathed in the cream that Gran would harvest from the top of the bottles for my cereal. There was always a rack of toast getting cold in the middle of the table, which they tried to convince me was the proper way to eat toast, but they were wrong about that, if only that. After the cereal, Gran would slide a plate of eggs, sausage, beans, tomatoes, and fried bread in front of me. Once that was devoured and washed down with a cup of tea, I was sent off to my room to study for a couple of hours. Gran would insist that I return at eleven o'clock for coffee and chocolate biscuits, and at one o'clock for a lunch of soup and pork pie or something similar. Then at four o'clock, there was tea, at seven there was supper, and then there was perhaps a few crisps (potato chips) before bed. What a place!

It was a magical time. Easter was late that year, April 19, and spring was well along. Every inch of ground seemed to be covered by my favourite flowers, daffodils, and I was living Wordsworth's 1804 poem that Marilyn had introduced to me:

I Wandered Lonely as a Cloud

I wandered lonely as a cloud
That floats on high o'er vales and hills,
When all at once I saw a crowd,
A host, of golden daffodils;
Beside the lake, beneath the trees,
Fluttering and dancing in the breeze.

Continuous as the stars that shine
And twinkle on the milky way,
They stretched in never-ending line,
Along the margin of a bay:
Ten thousand saw I at a glance,
Tossing their heads in sprightly dance.

The waves beside them danced; but they
Out-did sparkling waves in glee:
A poet could not but be gay,
In such a jocund company:

I gazed--and gazed--but little thought
What wealth the show to me had brought:

For oft, when on my couch I lie
In vacant or in pensive mood,
They flash upon that inward eye
Which is the bliss of solitude;
And then my heart with pleasure fills,
And dances with the daffodils.

Ted and I attended several services, Easter pageants, and bible studies over the two weeks. As one pastor was responsible for three churches in the area, we travelled to a different village or town for each event. However, the Good Friday service was held in the Mission Chapel in the Winters' own village, Blennerhasset. It was a soft day, warm and sunny, requiring only shirtsleeves as we walked arm in arm toward the church. They were singing hymns prior to the service. The place was full, the windows open, and as we approached, the voices of the faithful wafted out on the breeze to greet us:

Man of sorrows! What a name
For the Son of God, who came?
Ruin sinners to reclaim.
Hallelujah! What a Saviour!

Indeed, what a Saviour. My heart almost burst as the gloriously sunny day met with the ultimate glory of Easter, and that moment became for me an exercise in imagination in which one recalls to memory on those occasions when one wants to return to a place of solitude and peace.

The Winters were warm, generous, and gentle people, and I returned to the school feeling calm and confident about the challenges that lay ahead. Naturally, once we were all back at school, there was a certain level of tension pervading everything as people faced the impending exams and the reality that if one failed the first time, there would be only one more chance. Everyone knew someone who had failed in some previous year, and that seemed to loom over everyone's heads.

A week or two prior to the final exams, we were given a long weekend of four days. Almost everyone went home, all except us three Canadians, John—an Irish lad—and a South African girl in the year behind us. Wondering if the others might enjoy a meal of fish and chips, I went in search of them. Entering one of the common areas, I tripped over a suitcase near the door.

"Someone else not left yet?" I inquired.

There was a long moment of awkward silence. Then someone in the gathered group of foreign students spoke up. "We are going to the Isle of Wight for the weekend," she said.

"Who is we?" I inquired.

"All of us," she replied. That was when I realized that *all of us* meant the other two Canadians, John, and the South African. I will admit that I was shocked. There was no way they could have organized such a trip without discussing and planning it. Furthermore, in order for me not to know, they would have had to sworn each other to secrecy.

I said nothing and simply turned and left, heading in the direction of the fish and chip shop.

Shortly after I left the building, I heard footsteps running after me. It was John who, supposedly, felt a need to speak with me.

"What can I do for you, John?" This was not an unusual question, as I had, in the course of three years, done many things for John and several of the other students also.

"Ruth, we're friends, and you know that I love you."

"Actually, John, I don't know that."

"I do, and it's not that we didn't think about inviting you. It's just that if you came along, we would have to look after you, and then we wouldn't have as much fun."

Zing! These were shocking, hurtful words to me. Yes, I was the only totally blind person in the class, but I was also the most capable one in the group, the one everyone depended upon for just about everything: preparing a good meal, pressing their clothing before a date, organizing airline tickets home, or liaising with the principal to get the things we wanted or needed. The only thing I said to John was, "Go back and join the others. You don't want to miss your train."

Before turning back, John admitted that Sylvie had suggested I would be hurt, but the one thing they could count on from me was forgiveness. Later, while discussing the situation with Sylvie, I stated my disappointment that I so often had to exercise that forgiveness and that others wantonly took advantage of it, especially those who considered themselves my friends.

I spent the entire four-day weekend alone in the seven-storey building except for the manager and his family, who resided in the penthouse and whom I did not see, although I knew they were there. Once back at school, Gillian, the other Canadian, was confined to her bed with a nasty gastrointestinal bug she'd managed to pick up on the trip. I discovered her plight after inquiring about her, as I had not run into her in the usual places. Checking in on her, I found her lying in her bed in a mess of vomit and in no state to do anything about it. As I stripped and remade her bed and gave her a fresh nighty, I asked her where her friends were—the ones with which she had gone to the Isle of Wight. Of course, she said nothing.

As a totally blind physiotherapy student, one does not go unnoticed, although I was trying hard to fly under the radar of too much scrutiny. Prior to my cardiopulmonary surgery placement at Harefield, I had been warned by other students and qualified blind therapists that the senior supervising clinician was a strong opponent of blind people becoming physiotherapists and, if I were assigned to her, I should keep my head down and say little. When I informed everyone that I was assigned to Ann, they all said that I should expect to be treated harshly and would receive a poor evaluation.

Much to my surprise, I rather liked Ann. She knew her business, and I was there to learn from her and made a concerted effort to do so. One lunch hour, a staff member informed everyone that she had seen Paula Walker, the district superintendent of physiotherapy, who was responsible for several hospitals in the area. The tension in the staff room rose.

"She is tough," I was informed. "You don't want to be in her bad books."

When someone walked into the room and announced that Miss Walker wanted to speak with me, everyone froze. I was scared! Had a patient complained? Had Ann said something? I was shaking as I entered her office.

She had a gruff, less than feminine voice when she invited me to sit down. I found the chair and nervously slid into it.

"Miss Vallis," she began, "I hear you are a Canadian."

"Yes, ma'am."

She went on, "When I was a young therapist, I spent a year working at Victoria Hospital in Montreal. It was a wonderful year, and I should never have returned to England. Physiotherapy in Canada is a dynamic profession, and so are the therapists. Miss Vallis, I hear good things about you. I am told that you are a true Canadian and will fit in well in that dynamic environment."

I did not know what to say. I thanked her and returned to the staff room. Everyone was eager to find out what had happened behind the closed door, but I simply disclosed that she wanted to talk to me about Canada.

A few days prior to the final exams, I was summoned to Vice-Principal Marshall's office. "Miss Vallis, I have received a phone call from Ann at Harefield Hospital. Do you know who Ann is, Miss Vallis?"

"Yes sir, she was my supervising therapist."

"Oh, Miss Vallis, she is much more than that. She is one of the most outspoken people against blind physiotherapists."

"Yes sir, I had heard that about her, but maybe I misunderstood something. I didn't have any trouble with her, and she gave me a good evaluation."

"Ruth, she called us about you, and she said this: 'If ever there was a blind person who could change my mind about the possibility of blind people becoming physiotherapists, it is Ruth.' Well done, my dear! We agree with her, but now you have to overcome the examination hurdle."

"I will give it my best shot, sir."

Laughing, he said, "Yes, I am sure you will. Ruth, if ever a blind person deserved to be a physiotherapist, it is you, but my heart bleeds for you. Getting the qualification is only the first obstacle. You will then have a lifetime of continuously convincing people you are worthy. It is not going to be easy, Miss Vallis, but we believe you are one of the five most capable blind people in the entire British Commonwealth and, if anyone can do it, you can."

The exams consisted of written papers in May and a practical exam in June. The night before the written exams, it felt as though everyone was about to explode. I found Michelle and Joanne and asked whether they would like to play nine holes of golf.

"Ruth, we have our part twos tomorrow!"

"Yes," I admitted, "but can you learn three years' work in one night? We either know it or not, and a couple more hours of cramming will not make any difference. In fact, it might cause confusion in our thoughts."

We took out our frustrations on some poor little golf balls and then picked up a takeout Chinese meal and just enjoyed a little distraction for a couple of hours. I shared with them a humorous letter of advice I had received from Mrs. Winter in which she instructed me on how to answer the exam questions. I don't recall everything she wrote, but I do remember this: "Read the question. Take a deep breath. Count to ten and then reread the question. Then answer the question the examiner has asked and not the question you wish the examiner had asked." We all had a big laugh over it but, indeed, it was sage advice.

The next morning, we gathered in the gymnasium where the invigilator spouted those familiar but obligatory rules, and then we were instructed to begin. The first paper was ten short answers, with which there was no choice. It covered all the subjects, such as anatomy, physiology, and physics. Oh yes, physics. We had to answer and pass each question individually, and it was only the physics question that caused me any angst. With Mrs. Winter's advice in my ears, I read the list of questions. I don't remember the other nine things asked, but I do remember the physics question: "For three marks, define buoyancy, streamline, and turbulence . . ."

A question on hydrotherapy! Thank you, God! Everyone, students and lecturers alike, were so expecting ultrasound that there was a collective moan when the others realized they had focused on the wrong topic. I left the gym uncertain that I had passed, but confident that I had a chance.

A month later, in preparation for the practical exam, I had my hair cut, bought new black leather shoes and new navy-blue trousers, and convinced the school housekeeper to give me a new crisp white tunic. Never certain how much influence my appearance would have on the examiners, I felt it necessary to look my professional best. We were divided into two groups, alphabetically. Half of us were examined on Monday, and I, being V, was the last to be examined on Tuesday. Those of us on the second day stayed well away from those who were examined on Monday so as not to get any more nervous than we were already. Furthermore, I gathered the Tuesday group together and made a full English breakfast for everyone so we would all be well fuelled for the task ahead. Once I arrived at the hospital, I was met by Miss Begg, who was orchestrating everything. She commented on my sharp appearance and said that she had heard about the breakfast.

There were three steps to completing the practical physiotherapy exam. The main component, and the one everyone was concerned about for me, was where I had to sit in front of a physician and physiotherapist and answer a series of questions based on a chart I had read and an actual patient I had assessed. I was calm, and my thoughts were clear and confident about everything and anything they asked me. The bell rang to signal the end of the twenty minutes, and Miss Begg came to get me. The examiners wanted to ask me another question, but Miss Begg declined on my behalf, stating that time was up and I had answered enough. Once away from the examiners, Miss Begg asked me what had happened.

I wasn't certain to what she was referring.

She said, "The anxiety."

"Oh, that," I chuckled. "I studied hard and prayed earnestly, and the Lord has honoured me with the clear thoughts and calm spirit for which I had asked."

"Ruth, if I were not already a Christian, I would be converted today based on the transformation in you." She then ushered me into a side room, gave me tea, chocolate biscuits, and cookies, and urged me to relax, for it was all over!

Shortly after that, I had to move out of the residence and, once again, I found myself needing a place to stay until the results came out at the end of July. Michelle and Joanne were sharing a flat around the corner from the school, and they generously invited me to occupy their couch. I eagerly accepted, as they were a lot of fun, and the food was good. In early July, we all attended the wedding of two classmates in Wales. While there, I took the opportunity to call Marilyn and update her on things. It was great to hear her voice, and she seemed delighted to hear mine. I informed her that I would be receiving my results in three weeks' time and was feeling guardedly hopeful.

Her voice was tender and encouraging when she said, "Come home, Ruth, and I will help you hang your shingle." Buoyed up, I returned to London to await July 27.

Like most students in history, we spent a lot of time in exam post-mortems. I felt confident about Michelle and Joanne, as they worked hard and seemed to have a good grasp of the profession. They suggested the same confidence in me. I hadn't scheduled my flight home, and they had planned to give up their flat and return to Yorkshire as soon as they knew they had qualified. Michelle challenged me to book my flight for the day after the results came out. Not a church person herself, she badgered me with "Where's your faith, Ruth?" I phoned Air Canada, explained my situation to the reservation woman and she, with words of encouragement, scheduled me on a flight for July 28. The next morning, we all awoke with anxiety-related gastrointestinal problems but managed to gather our wits sufficiently to stagger off to the school to get our results. We were not aware that those who were not successful had already been awakened very early by a courier who had hand-delivered the bad news.

As Michelle, Joanne, and I entered the school, Principal Teager's office door was wide open. Spotting us, he jovially shouted, "You three, get in here!" I leaned against the wall so as not to fall over. "Miss Vallis, today you are a physiotherapist, and well deservedly so!"

"Did everyone pass, Sir?" I asked.

His reply was simply, "You should know better than to ask that."

We all gathered in the lounge for a sandwich and celebratory glass of wine. Mr. Field spoke of his pride for all of us and, especially me. He suggested that I return home, open a private practice, and send for him to come and work for me.

"Sir, I have only one question."

"Yes, Miss Vallis?"

"Sir, can you sing?" Touché!

That evening, the whole class got together for one last dinner. It was there that we learned that two had not passed, John being one. Walking along afterwards, John came alongside me, put his arm around me, and congratulated me on my success. "You must be very proud of yourself," he said.

"Yes, I am pleased, but I would feel better if everyone had succeeded. You see, John, there is no more glory."

"No," he said. "I deserved that."

The next day, I went to Heathrow for the final journey home. A classmate, Penny, accompanied me. I was used to travelling alone, but she didn't want me to be alone this time. I must admit I was glad for her company. I had flown back and forth so many times over the three years that the staff at Air Canada knew me well. At check-in, I was greeted by name. When the woman behind the counter asked whether I was on my way home for another vacation, Penny corrected her. "Ruthy qualified yesterday, and she is on her way home for good."

"Congratulations!" the woman offered with great enthusiasm. Penny and I parted, and I headed for the plane. Every Air Canada employee from that moment on congratulated me. At the gate, I was informed that I was moving to business class, compliments of the airline. During the flight, I was invited up to the cockpit, where the captain also offered his congratulations. Apparently, Air Canada had an efficient line of communication that was working particularly well on that occasion. At home, my parents, brothers, and Marilyn were waiting to greet me and celebrate my achievement.

CHAPTER 14

The physiotherapy training had been very demanding, and I well understood those of my classmates who had decided to travel and have some fun before settling into their jobs and work routines. However, Joanne and Michelle had interviews as soon as they had their qualifications, and I hoped for the same good fortune. As it had been my dream from childhood to work in a hospital, that was my first choice. However, there were only two hospital jobs open in Toronto, and both were looking for senior therapists—one in pediatric rehab and the other in respiratory care. It is just as well that I wasn't qualified, because I wasn't interested in those areas. Although Mr. Field had suggested I open a clinic, I wasn't interested in working in a clinic, but those were the only jobs going at the time.

I applied at Humber Physiotherapy. It was a relatively small clinic and only about a thirty minutes' journey on the subway and bus from my parents' home. I was interviewed by the owner. She offered me the position on the spot, which I accepted happily. Once one is employed, one has to inform the licensing board, and the clinic owner said that she would also be letting them know of my new employment. I was asked to arrive at eight in the morning on September 4 to begin my first day. I was thrilled and excited. Peach was delighted for me and bursting with pride. She loved to repeat, "My daughter is a physiotherapist," and now I was an employed one.

I arrived bright and early on Tuesday, eager to dig in. Like every other newly qualified professional, I believed I could conquer the world and wanted to prove it. Upon entering the reception area, I was met with a cool and awkward atmosphere. The secretary, the owner's daughter and not a physiotherapist, informed me that the owner wanted to speak with me first thing. As I entered the boss's office, I knew something was wrong.

Without even offering me a seat, she simply said, "You can't work here."

I almost fell over. "But you have already employed me. What has changed?"

She ushered me into the treatment area and asked me how I would manage the equipment. I informed her that I was trained and qualified to work with this equipment.

"How would you know the dials were in the right place?"

"They are slightly tactile," I said, "and I can put some transparent Braille numbers on them to be extra certain."

"No, no. You can't work here!" I was escorted to the door that was closed quickly behind me. I had been hired and fired without one single minute of working. Stunned, I started to cry and didn't try to fight the tears. I cried all the way home but, as I sat on the subway, I prayed, remembering the scripture from Matthew 10:14, which says, "If anyone will not welcome you or listen to your words, leave that home or town and shake the dust off your feet." With my heart broken, I asked God to help me put this behind me and to accept that it was not the job he had in mind for me. Nevertheless, Vice-Principal Marshall's words were coming true. I might always have to struggle for acceptance and constantly prove myself.

Peach was surprised to see me home so soon. I explained what had happened and, like any loving parent, she was hurting for me but could do nothing but offer comfort. I had told everyone that I had a job, and now I had to tell them that I no longer did. Marilyn asked me whether I was certain I had been given the job, but that question deserved no answer, especially as the clinic owner had informed the licensing board. I needed no greater proof. Some people urged me to launch a wrongful dismissal lawsuit, suggesting that this could be my opportunity to own a clinic—that one! No, I was not going to sue or embarrass the woman. I had asked God to help me shake the dust in faith that he had something much better in store for me.

Peach opened the newspaper and started reading through the want ads again, but nothing jumped out at us. However, two days later, I received a most interesting phone call. The voice on the other end identified herself as one of the owners of Shelton Physiotherapy and Associates clinic. She said that she had heard I was looking for a job, and they were looking for a physiotherapist to replace someone who was leaving at the end of the week.

I asked how she knew about me and how she'd gotten my contact information. She explained that there was a therapist named Robby who worked part-time at Shelton's who also worked at Humber Physio. He shared with the Shelton management that there had been a meeting of the staff at Humber to inform them that a new therapist had been hired and that she was blind. According to Robby, who was present for the meeting, there were some concerns raised by the staff, but much of the protesting, and there was a lot, came from the secretary, the owner's daughter. Robby felt it unfair and unprofessional and suggested that Shelton Physio should offer me their upcoming vacancy. Hence, I was called to come in for an interview.

Shelton and Associates was a very large clinic situated in the basement of a shopping centre. They opened at seven in the morning and closed at nine in the evening. They had at least eight full- and part-time therapists, two assistants, and three receptionists.

I was offered the job, and I accepted. The salary was reasonable, but it had no benefits and was lots of hard work. They did good work, and I learned from some of the more experienced staff.

My hours were eleven in the morning to seven at night, which I didn't like, but it was suggested that if another slot came available, I would be kept in mind for it. A perfect schedule of seven to three came open, but I was passed over, as it was an easier schedule to fill than mine. The only perk in my hours was that many patients who were scheduled for the late afternoon appointments would feel sorry for me having to work at dinner hour. The clinic was in a predominantly Italian neighbourhood, and I was skinny, so patients would often arrive with hot chocolate, doughnuts, pizza, or any number of wonderful treats.

We had a receptionist, Joan, a big woman with a loud voice, who wore a fragrance not unlike insect repellent and went to the hairdresser weekly. She had been married three times but had no children. If a patient arrived late, she would snap instructions about punctuality at them. If they complained about having to wait, she would bark orders to sit down and shut up. She could often be heard letting fly with a string of ear-stinging four letter words. One might wonder how she maintained her position, but she was good at her job, and Mrs. Shelton probably depended upon her to keep things running smoothly. I loved her. She was everything I did not want to be, but I admired her big personality and take-no-prisoners approach to life. She was always kind to me. She greeted me warmly and would go out of her way to help me in every way possible, which often meant lining up pages from the patients' charts in my typewriter to ensure I documented accurately on the correct person. She was determined that no one found fault with me and never attribute an error to my being blind. A couple of times, she took me to lunch, much to the disapproving gossip of some other staff and management, and upon her return from a trip to California, she proudly presented me with souvenirs.

Joan was a bit of a coconut. She had a hard, rough exterior but a sweet, soft centre. She was about sixty and didn't drive, but she took the train from Toronto to London, approximately two hours, every third weekend to visit an elderly uncle. She did his food shopping, cooking, laundry, and a few other chores before returning home and back to work and, believe it or not, she sang in a church choir.

One day, Joan didn't show up for work. She had never been late, so it was a bit of a surprise. Everyone was planning what they would say when she finally did arrive, although they admitted they might not have the nerve once faced with the opportunity. The patients were also surprised not to see, or hear her, at the reception desk and were eager to tell her about the importance of punctuality or to sit down and . . . Management phoned her apartment, but there was no answer. We waited a couple more hours, but then became very concerned. The superintendent of her building was alerted and asked to check and see if she was okay. Not long after that, we received the very sad news that Joan had died in her bed during the night.

At the funeral, Joan's sister-in-law from California sought me out. She was eager to tell me how much Joan loved me. She recounted how, while on vacation, Joan was determined to find gifts that were textured or shapes I could easily identify by touching. She thought of me as the daughter she always wished she'd had.

Although Shelton's was one of the better clinics in Toronto at the time, it was still a bit of a therapy factory, and I was starting to have regular headaches and resent the schedule. Robby left to start his own clinic and asked me whether I would be interested in coming to manage it for him, as he hoped to open more than one in under-serviced areas of the city. I wasn't interested, but thanked him for his confidence in me from day one.

One morning in April, Pat, the most junior of the associates and the one I knew the least, took me aside for a private conversation. "Ruth, I wanted to let you know that there is a physiotherapist job posting for Hillcrest Hospital. Don't take this as me wanting to get rid of you. In fact, you are one of the best physios we have ever had here, but you can do better. Hillcrest is a rehabilitation hospital with a good reputation, and there would be more opportunities for learning with a wider variety of patients and more opportunities to use your skills. It will be very difficult to replace you, so please don't tell the other owners that I gave you this information."

I thanked her profusely and have kept her secret—until now.

I don't know what it was about receptionists in those days, but Hillcrest also had a peculiar one. She had a propensity for getting the extension wrong whenever she patched through a phone call. If one asked to be connected to the head of a particular department, one could almost be certain that there would be no correlation between the requested person and the one who answered the phone. However, on the day that I called, I asked to speak to the one in charge of physiotherapy, and she got it right, even though I got her title wrong. When Joan Bartlett answered, I explained that I was inquiring about the physiotherapy position advertised in the newspaper.

"Can you come in Thursday morning at seven thirty for an interview?" she asked.

"Yes, but first I want to tell you that I am blind."

Without taking a breath she said, "So I will see you at seven thirty."

Although I had been to Hillcrest to sing as a teenager with my youth group, I wasn't certain how to get there. Peach offered to accompany me and, although I didn't think showing up with my mother would make the best impression, I accepted, and away we went, arm in arm.

Peach waited in the lobby while Joan escorted me to her office. It was a typical interview with all the standard questions. At the end, I was given an opportunity to ask anything on my mind, but I was more concerned that they know they could ask me about how I manage safely and competently as a physiotherapist who is blind.

Joan's reply was, "If you are good enough to qualify as a physiotherapist, then you are good enough to be employed as one." Although refreshing, I was a little taken aback by the unusually open-minded thinking. While I was in the interview, Peach read a notice on the wall that described National Volunteer Week asking the reader to consider being a volunteer in that hospital. Peach decided that if I landed the job, she would apply. She saw that as a gesture of support for me and an opportunity to see more of each other or perhaps be there if I needed her.

Wisely, before offering me the job, Joan met with the staff, informing them that the candidate she favoured was blind and, if she employed me, I would require some practical support from the rest of them with regard to reading and writing in patient charts, among other things. It was a mature and experienced staff, and they agreed to be of assistance wherever necessary. A few days later, Joan called and offered me the position. I was ecstatic. I finally had an in-patient hospital job, my lifelong dream. Peach had also been accepted as a volunteer patient porter for two half-days per week.

Each morning, the occupational and physiotherapy staff gathered to sort out the day ahead. On that first day, not a coffee drinker at the time, I accepted a glass of orange juice and an Arrowroot biscuit. As I took the first sip, I was met harshly with that familiar acidic, metallic taste typical of juice from a can. All the feelings I had as a child in quarantine came flooding back to me, but then I realized I was not the little girl alone and confined to a metal crib but, rather, a woman with the freedom that being an educated professional brings.

CHAPTER 15

After living away from home in England, it was never my intention to move back into my parents' house. Of course, initially, I had nowhere else to go, and Peach encouraged me to not be in a hurry to be out on my own. By that time, my parents were retired, and I could come home to a cooked meal. They were very concerned, especially Dad, that I was doing too much between the church and the hospital, and they wanted to relieve me of some daily responsibilities.

Although I had managed to navigate London, England (including the underground), with a white cane and was doing well at home, I thought getting around Toronto might be even easier and less stressful with a guide dog. I spoke to my parents about it, and they both said no. Peach and Dad were both great animal lovers, and we had always had pets, but they knew a young woman in the neighbourhood who had a guide dog, and they would often see her at the local mall sitting on a bench with a very tight grip on the dog's collar and leash. They felt it was an unhappy life for the dog and would, therefore, not agree to have one in their house. So, I pushed the thought to the back of my mind and continued tapping along with my cane. Interestingly, there were two subsequent incidences where a dog might have made a difference.

One morning as I was leaving for work, I crossed our street directly in front of the house and headed north toward the bus stop. A car drove slowly along beside me and stopped. The car doors opened, and people stepped out. I noticed but didn't think anything of it. However, at the same time, Peach was upstairs in the bathroom getting washed when she suddenly had a feeling that compelled her to rush downstairs and say goodbye to me one more time. Upon opening the door, she saw two men slowly approaching me from behind. "Goodbye, honey," she yelled. "Have a good day."

With that, the two men looked up, saw her, quickly retreated to their car, and hastily drove away. Peach stayed there and watched me until she could no longer see me and did so every day for a long time after that.

Women walking alone in the early morning or late evening are vulnerable, and the common advice is to always be aware of one's surroundings. Although I have always considered myself to be an alert person, blindness limits one's ability to perceive everything in one's surroundings and adds an extra layer of vulnerability.

I was learning a great deal from my colleagues who took a sincere interest in helping me develop as a clinician; I was still quite green when I started at Hillcrest. One of Joan's important and helpful pieces of advice was that the threshold of the hospital was a necessary dividing line. One must learn that when one enters the hospital, one must leave personal matters outside. By the same token, when one leaves the hospital, one must leave work issues inside. This piece of advice, combined with Miss Begg's advice that I temper my love with professionalism, led me to develop a personal policy that patients were not friends. For the most part, this was not a huge conflict. However, on one occasion, I had a male patient who was not much older than myself. He asked me if, once he was discharged, could he take me out to dinner. I thanked him but said no. He persisted, and I resisted. He protested, saying that we were friends. I explained that our relationship was purely professional, and that he must not confuse my friendliness with friendship. I was glad when he was discharged, but about a month later, he returned to visit me. He had been on a trip to Florida and came bearing gifts of clothing and perfume. I told him that I couldn't accept them, turned down another dinner invitation, and asked him to stop visiting me.

A short while later, a woman who waited at the same bus stop with me every morning happened to mention that there was a man sitting in a car across the street looking at me. She said he was often there and thought

I should know. I wasn't certain who it was, and I had no way of knowing that he was even looking at me until he started sitting in his car outside my home and one evening yelled out, "Have dinner with me!" That was the beginning of months of stalking. The phone calls were bad enough, but knowing that he was watching me—but never knowing where or when—was very creepy and frightening. Stalking was not yet a common topic of conversation, nor was it in the news, and informing the police was not even a consideration, as I didn't know what I would say. "Someone is phoning me, and I think they are watching me, but I don't know when and I don't know where?"

As a child, I listened to the Audrey Hepburn film Wait Until Dark. I found the silent pursuit of a blind woman incredibly disturbing and, for years, I would not even let the memory of that movie come to mind; yet here I was, a blind woman being silently pursued. In the film, Audrey Hepburn gets the upper hand after dark when she destroys any access to lights for her stalker. I didn't have that advantage. A couple of times, Peach noticed him sitting out front in his car and, annoyed for me, told him that I was not interested and to be on his way.

Fortunately, after a few months, it suddenly stopped. I don't know whether he just got tired of it or whether he had fallen ill again. Frankly, I didn't care which, as long as it ceased. Peach suggested that Dad could walk me to and from the bus stop every day if that would make me feel more comfortable, but I declined the offer. It was too restrictive, and I would have rather had a dog.

Hillcrest was a great hospital for me on many levels. It was small, only four floors with, initially, 117 beds. Everyone knew everyone, and there was great care for the patients and for each other.

We had a British physio on staff named Chris Long. She had excellent knowledge and skills and was eager to share them with me. She would read interesting articles to me from physiotherapy journals, wanting to help me stay current while emphasizing the need to do so. Furthermore, if she had a patient with an especially rare or complicated diagnosis, she would talk me through her choice of treatment and reasons for her approach. When reading my patient charts to me, which she did often, she would point out significant details that I should pay close attention to and why.

There is no greater inspiration than success, and as my knowledge and skills increased, so did my confidence. My passion for physiotherapy and the work we did at Hillcrest grew exponentially. I was treating multiple traumas, total joint replacements, and various fractures. In order to ensure the smooth management of patient care, the therapy sessions were kept to a regular schedule, which suited me very well. There were two therapy gyms, and I was assigned to the smaller one. This allowed me to move freely and safely in and out and between the plinths. I didn't have to worry about tripping over other therapists, their patients, or their equipment. My assistants—I had several over the years—kept the place tidy, and we always returned equipment to where it belonged so that I could reach out and grasp whatever I needed without fumbling about. It was always important to me to appear competent and dignified. I did not want anyone, especially patients, to feel sorry for me or question my ability to do the job. To this end, I received an enormous compliment one day when a patient in my gym referred to someone up on the ward as my sister. I explained that she must be mistaken, as I didn't have a sister. She thought it uncanny, as the woman looked exactly like me. I suggested that it was me.

"No," she said, "this woman is blind and walks around the ward with a white cane."

My greatest pleasure of the day was being in the pool. Yes, Hillcrest had a therapy pool, and I took patients in the water for hydrotherapy treatments for an hour every day, but it was also an enormous blessing to me personally. Although I hadn't had any trouble with my rheumatoid joints since childhood, I was starting to have some knee swelling again and, by exercising the patients and myself in the water regularly, I was able to stay flexible and strong.

One of the articles Chris read to me discussed the high rate of suicide in the physiotherapy profession. The predominant reason was pain. Patients come in pain, and they either have or expect pain during the treatment. I could understand the statistic to a degree, as I found dealing with pain—offering support and encouragement while trying to mobilize patients who were screaming in pain or paralyzed with fear—to be the most challenging aspect of the job. Although I acknowledged patients' pain and did my best to manage it through effective treatments, I dealt with it in two ways for my own sake and the sake of the other patients being treated at the same time: I used humour and distraction through the discussion of current events.

I had a few rules for the smooth running and comfortable atmosphere of my treatment sessions. I did not allow patients in the gym or the pool to give organ recitals. That is, they were not permitted to list all their kidney, liver, heart, etc. problems or try to one-up each other with their number of diseases or surgical procedures. I would say, facetiously, that the only things they could talk about were sex, politics, or religion. Other patients or staff would often ask why there was so much laughter coming from my gym, and I would ask them what they would prefer.

With few exceptions, people loved the pool. It was warm, made movement easier for everyone, and helped in the reduction of swelling and pain. Patients would say that they felt so much better after a hydrotherapy treatment, and I would reply, "That is because you have been to the fountain of Ruth." We had so much fun in the water. There was plenty of serious treatment, but the psychological benefits were immeasurable. Once in a bathing suit, the pool has a way of levelling the playing field. However, I had to be very sensitive to cultural and religious differences and encourage some women to wear long T-shirts over their suits for modesty or stagger the treatment sessions to prevent women and men from being in the water together. Occasionally, after realizing the improvement they felt, some would forgo the cover-up or gender divide.

As I was always singing—no, Mr. Field, I did not get fired for insubordination—I would encourage the patients to join me. One of the less-enforced rules was that patients were to sing us a song on their last day. Few ever declined. They would often sing, "So Long, It's Been Good to Know Yuh," but occasionally, someone would be prepared and waiting for their moment. One very memorable singing performance came from an Italian gentleman. He was quiet and very focused on his exercises. As he was departing the water on his last day, he asked if I wanted him to sing. I was a little surprised at his eagerness, but happily urged him on. Needless to say, the acoustics in the pool were exceptional, and he took full advantage. We were all stunned as his glorious voice filled the place with beautiful music.

He laughed at our surprised expressions. "I didn't tell you," he admitted impishly. "I was a professional opera singer in Italy."

It was not always so easy. One of my colleagues had a patient who was very difficult to treat. Apparently, she found the hospital a pretty comfortable place, and every time the staff thought they were on top of her problem, she would come up with something else that she felt needed attention. Her symptoms were always vague and her cooperativeness challenging. She was treated in the large gym and would often just scream at the top of her lungs, and the reasons were never clear. She did nothing for herself, as she denied that she was able to do anything. Eventually, her physiotherapist transferred her into my care. Sometimes, a fresh approach can identify things that have been overlooked. It was also felt that the less busy, smaller gym might be more conducive to her recovery.

She agreed to the therapist and venue change, so I assisted her onto the plinth and, after a brief review of her diagnosis, I explained the treatment. Thorough education has always been at the core of my interaction with patients, long before it was popular or mandated. I have never believed that ignorance is bliss—Peach's influence, without a doubt. This woman seemed to appreciate the information or perhaps the extra attention. Anyway, I started her on her exercises and then moved on to others in the gym. Suddenly, the woman let out a blood-curdling scream. I rushed over to attend to whatever was the issue.

"What is wrong?" I asked.

"I have pain," she answered calmly. She was there because of a left-knee surgery. I touched her knee, but she said, "No, it's my shoulder." I touched her shoulder and she said, "No, I mean my right ankle."

"Does any of this have anything to do with your left knee?" I asked.

"No, it is my back."

"Okay, let me get this straight. Where is the pain specifically?"

"Don't you understand I have pain?" she snapped irritably. The other patients were getting restless.

"Ma'am, I understand that you have pain, and I will do my best to help you, but I need to understand where it is so I can determine what is causing it and then select the best treatment for you. However, you cannot scream in here."

"Screaming helps me," she said.

"It may help you, but it doesn't help the other patients, and it doesn't help me."

"Maybe the other patients aren't in pain," she sniffed.

"Oh yes, they are," I said. "I make sure of it."

With that, all the others burst out laughing. Giving her a little space, I left her to attend to one of the others and, while my back was turned, the woman who was in agony and could do nothing for herself jumped off the plinth, put on her shoes, and ran out the door. She rushed back to her room, packed her case, and left the hospital. It was considered by all to be a miracle.

I believe that a successful society is both an educated and healthy society and, therefore, I am a staunch proponent of both public education and a public health-care system. As holy ground, every person has the right to education and health care in order to reach their potential and be able to contribute in a meaningful way back to society as a whole. However, as public health care is occasionally seen as a free service, which it is not, there are those who treat it with little regard. Consequently, another one of my rules, for which I was very well known, was punctuality.

I believed that the patients should regard their rehabilitation as a job. They should arrive on time and give their all. In my initial meeting with every patient, I would always say, "I will do my best for you, but I also expect you to do your best for you." Furthermore, if people were late for their appointments, it would impact my whole schedule and the treatment time of others.

Sadly, there are many in this world for whom structure and taking responsibility are not a concern. One such person became my patient early on in my career. We'll call him Fred. I think he fell off a bicycle. He was thirty-something, never worked, had no ambition—not even to shower, clean his teeth, or change his clothing. An unlucky chap, he became my patient and, being younger and fitter than some of my older patients, I assigned him the 9:00 a.m. slot along with two or three others.

Every morning, Fred was late for treatment. Breakfast was served by eight, so I knew he was awake and should have been on time. Every day, as he sauntered in fifteen to thirty minutes late, I would remind him of the time of his appointment. One day, frustrated, I explained to him that when Mickey's big hand was on the twelve and his little hand was on the nine, his butt was to be on the plinth. The other patients giggled, but Fred said nothing.

A couple of days later, I had a meeting that went a few minutes after nine. As I walked into the room, I heard a commotion coming from the direction of Fred's plinth. For the first time, he had been punctual. I went over and said good morning, and he replied that he was leaving. According to him, if he had to be on time, then I also had to be on time. I admitted that I was a few minutes late and apologized, but explained that I had been in a meeting with management and left as soon as I was able. Fred insisted that the rules were for everyone and continued to gather his things to leave.

By then, it was no longer funny. "Fred, there are two kinds of people in this world: those who wait, and those for whom they are waiting. In this situation, Fred, I don't wait for you, but you will, if necessary, wait for me, and today is just such a day."

He continued to insist on leaving.

"Fred, if you walk out of this gym, then you just keep on going, because I will not treat you again. I will not tolerate disrespect for me, my profession, or the public health-care system."

Nevertheless, he walked out. I called his nurse and explained what had happened and, frustrated with him herself, she agreed and offered support.

The next morning, as I entered the gym, I greeted the patients. I suddenly became aware that someone was on Fred's plinth. I went over and there he was, early. "Good morning, Fred."

"Ah, ah, hi, Ruth."

"Nice to see you, Fred."

"I am sorry about yesterday," he offered sheepishly.

"Apology accepted. All is forgiven," I replied.

Softly he asked, "Can I stay?"

"Of course, Fred. Let's make this the first day."

With that, he thrust a cold can into my hands and said, "I brought you an Orange Crush!" He was never late or disrespectful again.

That hospital became such a part of me that people started calling me Miss Hillcrest. However, I was also busy outside the hospital, often receiving requests to speak at various events and conferences.

In the summer of 1987, I spoke at a Peel Region seminar on the education and training of blind children and young adults. In attendance were professionals representing education and social work as well as blind children and their parents. During the question period, an Italian gentleman asked me, "What will happen to my Theresa? She is four years old, totally blind, and just stomps around the house all day."

I explained that she stomped around to hear the echo of her footsteps, which provided her with navigational input. She was learning to detect the size of the room and to find furniture by the way the sounds changed when she got farther or closer to large objects. She was learning to see, as it were, with her ears.

He persisted, wondering what would happen to her.

"Sir, we are living in wonderful times with increasing technology and opportunities—your Theresa can be just about anything she wants to be."

"No," he said, "I am a simple man, and Theresa is a simple child who is also blind."

"Sir, look at me. My father too is a simple man."

"But," he said, "there was only one Albert Einstein, one Sigmund Freud, and there is only one Ruth Vallis. What will happen to my Theresa?" Those words rang heavily in my heart. Peach was very aware that it was not going to be easy for me, and Vice-Principal Marshall warned me that I would have a struggle for acceptance out in the world, but the one thing I had was parents who believed in me, including a mother who was always in my corner.

I enjoyed the event, but once it was over, I moved on to other things. That is, until I received a phone call at work a couple of weeks later from a social worker who had heard my presentation. She stated that she had an unusual request. She explained that she was working with a Korean family with a four-month-old daughter, Elaine, who had been born blind. Apparently, in some groups of the Korean culture, it was believed that if a child was born with a disability, it was because the parents had sinned in some way and they were being punished. Furthermore, if the disability was blindness, it was the ultimate punishment for the worst sin, although one did not necessarily know what one had done. Elaine's mother, due to cultural embarrassment, did not want to keep her, and I was asked if I would adopt her. I couldn't believe my ears. Further discussion revealed that, although they were not concerned for the physical well-being of the child, they were very worried about her mother, as she was suicidal. Apparently, the rest of the family was of little help, as they too were struggling with the stigma of a blind child. I explained to the social worker that I had some thinking to do. Over dinner that night, I shared the call with my parents. They were surprisingly positive, but they agreed that I had to give it some serious consideration.

The next day, my parents asked if they could talk to me about Elaine. They had obviously discussed it at great length and had a plan. They said that if I adopted her, they would help me by looking after her while I was at work and in any other ways necessary. My parents were in their mid-sixties, and I asked whether they really wanted to be raising an infant at that stage in their lives. Dad assured me that they could manage it together and that they would do it for me and Elaine. Speaking about it with my brother Paul, he thought it a wonderful thing and that I would be a good role model for the child.

Well, I did think and pray about it, but I did not feel it acceptable for such old superstitious thinking to be perpetuated in Canadian society by way of taking the child away and allowing that family to go on with their lives as though Elaine did not exist. I could not rationalize within myself my lifelong striving to be accepted as a normal person who happened to be blind with allowing that family, in particular the mother, to treat their own blind child, as a pariah to be discarded. At least Theresa's father wanted to help her.

With the blessing of my parents, I declined to adopt her and encouraged the social worker and other mental health professionals to continue working with the mother and family in the hopes that they would eventually shed themselves of superstitious and hateful thoughts. I was led to believe they were going to keep her and that positive headway was being made with her mother. Now decades later, I often wonder what and how she is doing. I am not sorry for the decision I made for myself, but there is a little pang of sadness as I wonder whether I made the right decision for Elaine. Was she sent away to board at the School for the Blind?

Many blind children are now integrated into the public school system. In fact, the School for the Blind in Vancouver, British Columbia, closed as a result. The provincially run W. Ross MacDonald School in Ontario continues, but with a greater focus on blind/deaf children. Unfortunately, I am not certain that integration has had the effect people might have hoped.

According to the National Federation of the Blind, one in nine visually impaired people in Canada and the US have no usable vision. Only 10 percent of those people read Braille. Of course, accessible computers and smart phones have made life much easier, but it is not literacy and, again, in Canada and the US, there is 80 percent unemployment among blind and visually impaired people. The more telling statistic is that of the 10 percent who read Braille, 80 percent are employed. There is an undeniable correlation between Braille literacy, higher education, and employment.

I gave a presentation to a master's degree class studying to be teachers of the blind at the University of Western Ontario. I started my presentation by saying, "If you are teaching your blind children to read and produce Braille, I congratulate you! However, if you are not, then you are a failure as a teacher!"

One of the men at the back of the room yelled out, "Controversial!"

"No, sir," I explained. "Braille is literacy for the blind, and if teachers don't insist on literacy, who will?"

Does Elaine know how to read Braille? Is she educated?

CHAPTER 16

For the first one hundred years of her existence, Hillcrest was exclusively an in-patient rehab hospital. Any patients requiring ongoing therapy on discharge were referred to other hospitals with out-patient departments or private clinics. However, increasing demands upon out-patient therapy meant long waiting lists, if they were accepting new patients at all. Furthermore, some hospital out-patient departments were only accepting referrals for people who were under the care of the doctors in that hospital, which frequently left Hillcrest staff in a predicament. Consequently, Joan decided that we needed our own out-patient program, and a proposal was presented to the board of governors, who embraced it eagerly.

The program began with physiotherapy offered two evenings per week, which quickly became four evenings. However, it was funded from the general budget as a pilot project with no external financial support. The initial cost was $40,000 annually—not an enormous sum, but most funds were already earmarked for the long-established programs.

By the time the program was two years old, it was running daily, and treatments started at one in the afternoon. We were taking our own discharged patients as well as community referrals, and we were obviously meeting a great need.

As health care is publicly administered, hospitals are not permitted to go over budget and run a deficit. Unfortunately, in 1988, Hillcrest Hospital did just that, possibly for the first time. As a result, it became necessary to find cuts within the budget. All the therapists were called into a meeting, although most did not know why. As we entered the room, a colleague, Katie Lundon, suggested that I listen but say nothing, waiting until we had all the information. Apparently, Katie knew what was coming down the pipe and was devising a plan.

At the front of the room stood Joan and the hospital president, L. Muldoon. Mr. Muldoon announced that, as the out-patient department had been funded from the general budget, they had to cancel the out-patient program. The room was quiet. Mr. Muldoon was obviously feeling awkward, especially with the silence. "Are there no questions?" he asked. Joan was emotional, and we felt for her, but we said nothing, like Katie had requested. The meeting ended, and everyone dispersed.

The physiotherapists had always been Mr. Muldoon's fair-haired girls— cooperative, supportive, and agreeable. Furthermore, it had been a very paternalistically run organization. Consequently, he may have felt a little powerless at our lack of response, and he wasn't used to that. I'm sure he wanted someone to say that we understood, but that wasn't going to happen. Poor chap! The times were changing, and he was about to find out by just how much.

Katie cornered me and asked, "Ruth, what do you think about us riding your tandem to save the program?" She suggested that we speak to her father, a physician and the head of internal medicine at a hospital in downtown Toronto, and run the idea past him. Katie and I explained to him that closing the out-patient department was not a solution, as we were offering an important service at a fiscally responsible rate. He encouraged us to try, congratulated us for our enthusiasm, but cautioned us to approach it without emotion: "Be the professional women you are."

We heard Dr. Lundon's advice and took it to heart because we knew he was right. We were embarking upon a major uphill challenge. This was not simply the physiotherapists begging Mr. Muldoon to reconsider: we were out to get full funding from the Ministry of Health, and that was going to take a salient argument and public pressure.

Peach gave us her blessing with the encouraging words, "If anyone can do this, it is you two."

With that, Katie and I made our pact to fight until we won full ministry funding.

Although funding to hospitals comes from the provincial Ministry of Health, there are transfer payments to the provinces from the federal Medicare program. Therefore, we decided to start our cycling trip on Parliament Hill in Ottawa and take a five-hundred-kilometre, five-day route to Hillcrest Hospital in Toronto. It was to be "One hill of a trip." However, there would be no point to this if we were the only ones who knew about it, and so Katie contacted local news programs. The story quickly caught on. Citytv named us the Dynamic Duo and followed our progress from beginning to end. Soon, the Canadian Physiotherapy Association wanted an interview to share with therapists across the country. The public started sending in donations to the hospital with letters and phone calls to the Ministry of Health.

On Thursday, August 18, 1988, at nine in the morning, Katie and I mounted my tandem and set off from Parliament Hill with Hillcrest's Member of Parliament, Barbara McDougall, waving us on our way. It must not have made a great impression on Ms. McDougall, because when I had occasion to meet her years later, she had no idea who I was nor any recollection of the event. She asked me to remind her what it was about and after the review, she replied, "Oh, I must be nice." Politicians!

We stayed in bed and breakfasts the first three nights and then with the sister of a colleague for the last one. People could not do enough for us. They gave us dinner when we arrived, hearty breakfasts before leaving, and snacks, drinks, and lunch to pack in the panniers for later. At one point, we were met, unexpectedly, on the highway by a married couple. One was a newspaper journalist, and the other was a newspaper photographer. They were not just there to cover our story, but were also prepared with refreshments—a sort of genteel, Canadian-style paparazzi.

On a couple of occasions, some colleagues came to meet us along the way, which was very psychologically helpful. Although the weather was perfect and we were cycling alongside lovely lakes and farms, there were long stretches of empty highway. Undoubtedly, folks at home were thinking of us, but one could easily feel alone and forgotten. I had a radio along for the ride, but the great Canadian Shield's solid granite did not allow for regular reception. Katie was entertaining as she spoke to the cows and sheep in the fields along the way and kept me informed of where we were at all times, including which intersection or new road we were looking for next. As each day drew to an end and I became tired, Katie would encourage me by saying, "Ruth, I can see the signpost!" Well, if Katie didn't have the best vision of anyone in the world, I didn't know who had any better. I swear she could see the sign from ten kilometres away. It always seemed to be a long stretch between when she announced she could see the signpost and when we actually came upon it, and sometimes, that sign was only the indicator of where we were to turn to head off in quest of another signpost.

The third day was especially difficult. Despite it being a late August weekend and with our passing numerous lakes that must have had cottages on them, we didn't pass any people or vehicles for hours. It was hot, and the air was still. We said nothing for a long time. Although I could smell the roadside grasses baking in the sun, it was rather like peddling in a vacuum. One does get lost in one's thoughts, but after many miles, one's mind tends to go numb, and time stands still. Suddenly, it felt like we were the only two people in the world. I wondered what Peach was doing at that moment. I asked, "Katie, do you think anyone is thinking about us right now?"

"Feeling lonely, Ruth?"

"Yes," I replied. "What about you?"

"Me too," she answered wistfully, and without another word, we simultaneously kicked the tandem into high gear and took off flying down the highway to make our next destination and call home.

That night, Peach's voice was light and encouraging. "How are you two girls doing, sweetie? We are all thinking about you and praying for you, and we can't wait until you are home safe and sound." Of course she was thinking of us. How could I have thought anything else?

It was Monday, August 22, when we turned down the last road toward the hospital. Suddenly, a car pulled up behind us with its horn blowing, driven by my mentor, Chris.

"Ruth," Katie yelled above the din, "that car is flying a huge bunch of balloons!"

As we turned into the hospital driveway, the physiotherapists and occupational therapists were holding an archway of crossed crutches and canes. We cycled under the arch and right through a Welcome Home banner into the parking lot where all the patients were sitting around the periphery with noise makers and balloons flying from their walkers and wheelchairs. We were greeted by staff, media, and Peach. Laurel wreaths were placed upon our heads, and glasses of cold liquid were pressed into our hands. There was a great carnival atmosphere. Katie and I embraced, and everyone was pleased to see that we were still friends.

Once the trip was behind us, we could do little more than wait for a response from the Ministry of Health. Donations with congratulatory notes continued to arrive for several days. The final total was $8,200, which was a goodly sum, more than we ever expected, and it could be used to buy new equipment for the program if the ministry agreed to fund it.

A week or two later, Mr. Muldoon sought me out. His uncomfortableness was very apparent as, while he stood talking to me, he kept putting one foot up on a chair and then the other. He repeated this nervous dance the entire time. "Ruth, we have had a phone call from the office of the Minister of Health, Frances Lankin. They have received numerous letters and phone calls pressuring them to fund our program. The message from Frances Lankin is that if this doesn't stop, they will shelve us."

I became incensed! "Mr. Muldoon, I understand the need to be fiscally responsible, especially with public funds, and at no time, in any interview with the media, did I point a finger at the ministry or blame them for the need to cut back on funding. However, they have recently given $17 million for storefront addiction treatment centres, and we are simply asking for $40,000 to serve a need in our community. These are the folks who have paid their taxes and have given back to society—some of them veterans—and now the government can't find $40,000 to meet their needs? No, Mr. Muldoon, Mrs. Lankin is accountable to her constituents, and if she does not know that, I would be happy to tell her! I will not stop with a tandem cycling trip. No sir, I will pitch a tent on the steps of Queen's Park. If she is annoyed by the publicity and public pressure thus far, just wait until the newspaper headlines say, 'Blind Woman Forced to Sleep on Steps of Provincial Legislature by Minister of Health Lankin!'"

With that, Mr. Muldoon and I parted company.

I am sure he felt fairly certain I was not bluffing. Three days later, we received notice that we would be granted full funding for an out-patient physiotherapy program. Today, it has grown and expanded to include occupational therapy, nursing, social work, and much more. Currently, the program runs daily and employs over twenty staff at the Toronto Rehabilitation Institute.

Two months later, I was at a city-wide physiotherapy fundraising event when I ran into Pat, the junior partner at Shelton and Associates. She embraced me, stating how proud she was of me and the cycling trip. "We have the newspaper article on the wall in our waiting room and tell everyone that you used to work for us. I knew that you and Hillcrest would be a good fit."

I shared that I felt God had inspired her to tell me about the job, and she agreed I might be right.

CHAPTER 17

Although I took every opportunity to promote Hillcrest Hospital and became known as Miss Hillcrest, I had another great passion, which was the Toronto Blue Jays baseball team. During my last year in England, I once again had a boyfriend at home, a university science student named Patrick Rupnarain. He telephoned me every Saturday and, during baseball season, would report on how the Blue Jays were doing. I understood nothing of what he was saying. Consequently, once home for good, I began listening to the games and learning the rules so I would know what he was talking about, and so began my love affair with the game. Patrick was pretty nice too, but our lives went in different directions.

I attended fifteen games per season, taking different people with me each time. I loved to take those who preferred soccer or American football and turn them into baseball fans. There are few things in life more pleasant than a warm summer evening, Tom and Jerry providing a vivid description of all the action through my radio headphones, an ice-cold Coke, a sausage on a bun, and nine men on a diamond. Now *that* truly is this girl's best friend! As a result of my fanaticism, I was also known as Miss Blue Jay.

There were two incidences that shall forever be associated with baseball for me. The first one occurred in 1992, when the Jays were heading for their first World Series championship.

There were close to fifty thousand people in the SkyDome that evening. I don't remember who was with me, but I was sitting in the third seat from the aisle, and my friend was in the fourth. Shortly after the game had started, a couple sat beside us, the young man beside me. I was intent on the action on the field when I thought I felt something hit my lap. With tens of thousands of people around, one expects to get jostled or bumped, so I ignored it. Then I became aware that the chap beside me seemed to be trying to get my attention, although he was only making funny sounds. Then I realized that there was in fact something *in* my lap and, whatever it was, it was resting in my groin crease at the top of my thigh. As a blind person, I am very careful what I touch, as I fear harming my precious fingers. However, I had to find out what was going on, so I very gently and very quickly tapped my index finger on the object. A little perplexed, I touched it again, increasingly aware of the agitation of my next seat mate. I shuddered as I discovered it was warm. One more quick touch and I found a warm, long, cylindrical thing pressed into my groin. Suddenly, it dawned on me. It was a hot dog! Apparently, the young man had bitten into his hotdog and the wiener had propelled strategically out of the bun and into my lap. I gingerly picked it up between my thumb and forefinger and asked, "Does this belong to you?"

With that, he eagerly snatched it from me, shoved it back into the bun, and ate it.

I thought it odd that he would consume it after its adventure in Never Never Land, but then, with the price of dogs at the ballpark, it was likely too much of an investment to waste. My companion and I started to giggle, composed ourselves, giggled again, and so began our uncontrollable, seat-rocking laughter. I guess the young chap was a little embarrassed and, before the third inning was over, he and his lady friend were gone.

The next year, the Jays were back on the hunt for another World Series ring. Marilyn and I were given tickets to a playoff game by one of my patients. We were delighted to be there, as Marilyn has been a baseball fan much longer than I, and it was great to be at such an important game with someone who knew and loved the sport as much as I did—to say nothing of just being with Marilyn.

We were seated in the fifth row of the second level, right behind third base. Hall-of-famer Rickey Henderson, the base-stealing record holder, was up to bat. Two young men were seated behind us, but they had gone out for food, leaving a beer on the floor by their seat. Henderson hit a bullet of a ball that was fouled off toward the second level behind third base. The crowd of fans rose to catch it. I had no idea what was going on and was of two minds whether to rise also.

Suddenly, Marilyn grabbed the back of my head and shoved it down between my knees while yelling, "Get down!"

The rocketed ball skimmed over me and struck the beer on the floor behind me. Beer splashed all over me as the ball banged wildly all over the section until someone had a souvenir. It could only be described as frightening! I was very fortunate that Marilyn had been so quick, or I may have been very seriously injured as the trajectory of that very hard ball toward Miss Blue Jay was like a magnet to an iron shaving.

We still attend games, but now we rent a room in the hotel that overlooks the stadium and enjoy the sport in comfort and safety. The windows open wide, so I can still hear the crowd, smell the burnt popcorn, and yell at the umpire: "Have you ever thought of getting registered with the Canadian National Institute for the Blind?" or "Can I lend you a guide dog? You're not seeing well today!"

By the early nineties, most of the therapists who had been at Hillcrest when I arrived had left to work in other organizations. A popular manager also moved on and, as is often the case, many staff left around the same time. This meant that many of those individuals who had originally agreed to read and write patient charts for me were gone. I was, initially, a little worried that new staff might not agree to step into the breech; they were not obliged to, after all. However, I need not have been concerned, because God is faithful, and this was no exception. Some of the new staff were even more helpful than the previous ones, in particular, Barbara Lenehan.

Barbara, like Chris, was a very skilled and knowledgeable therapist. She moved quickly, and she had excellent time-management skills and sharp wit. Perhaps the most uncomfortable thing for a blind professional is to call upon other busy professionals for assistance. We all had enough of our own work to accomplish without having to do the work of others as well, and I despised the thought of being a burden. It was not long before Barbara recognized my need for help and, in a gesture of true kindness, became my regular chart reader and writer. There were others who would also assist from time to time, but Barbara never waited for me to ask.

Whenever she had a few minutes to spare, she would seek me out and offer her services. I think she may have even scheduled time for me into her day. Furthermore, just like Chris, she was very thorough and never missed an important detail in any chart, no matter how well hidden they were among the reams of information. This was enormously important to me. After all, if a detail were missed that could lead to a detrimental choice of treatment for a patient, I would be held responsible.

The popular manager was eventually replaced by Sally Fisher. Sally was very bright, well read, well educated, and a wonderful physiotherapist. However, she was sadly lacking in interpersonal skills. I learned invaluable clinical skills from her, but she would single out certain staff to challenge them unnecessarily and often, inappropriately. She tended to prey on the weak and, although I would not likely be described as weak—I am Peach's daughter, after all—she gave me a hard time and was sometimes down-right cruel.

Just before Christmas, I was wearing a reindeer head pin on my collar.

"What's that?" she snapped.

"It's one of Santa's herd," I replied.

"Oh, I thought it was a picture of you. Well, not quite you. It hasn't had its eyes gouged out yet." Away she stomped.

That stung, and I fought tears.

I could have filed a complaint with human resources, but it wasn't my style. I was certainly hurt by some of her comments, but I chose to forgive her and tried to focus on appreciating the opportunities for learning that she made available to me and the others. Nevertheless, my hurt was never lost on Peach. Whenever I arrived home from work, she always inquired about my day. Even if I didn't want to talk and just said that everything was fine, Peach would encourage me to sit down with her after dinner and discuss the day.

Peach somehow always knew exactly how to respond to me. On those days when she was certain that I was upset, no matter how hard I tried to hide it, she would urge me to talk to her about it. Sometimes, we would have a dialogue where she would make suggestions or offer alternative ways of looking at a situation, and yet, at other times, when I was deeply despairing, she would sit quietly and just let me go on and on. On those occasions, after I talked for an hour or two (didn't matter to her how long), she would always say, "Now, go up to your room, take some time aside with the Lord, and tomorrow will be a better day." And it always was. At other times, on those less intense days, she would make me laugh by saying, "Do you want me to go up to the hospital and beat up Sally?" But frequently, she would say, "Remember, Ruth, you were there before Sally, and you will be there long after her."

The physiotherapists and occupational therapists would gather in the occupational therapy room for lunch. We would talk about almost anything. Consequently, there was a great deal of laughter. One lunch hour, we were chuckling about some funeral home names that were, unintentionally, very humorous. The mood in the room changed quickly after Sally marched in and started making fun of church names, which was not funny. That led her to making disparaging comments about church-attending Christians, which was another of her hobbies. After we had all gone back to work, Sally, knowing Barbara didn't go to church and thinking she had an ally, said to her, "Aren't those Christians frail?"

"I don't know, Sally," replied Barbara. "I look at you, and I look at me, and I look at Joan, and I look at Ruth, and they seem to have a much better ability to cope with life than you or me."

Around the time of the Blue Jays first World Series championship in 1992, I became very ill. I went through many tests, but no specific diagnosis was ever found. In fact, on the day the Jays finally won the series, I was not conscious and, therefore, unaware for a day that my beloved team were city heroes. Around the same time, it had come to my attention that there was an advanced hydrotherapy course being offered in Bath, England. Sally and Joan encouraged me to take it and, after getting the staff to agree, offered the whole physiotherapy education budget for the year to pay the tuition if I were accepted.

I mentioned to my doctor that I was applying for a course in England and wanted to know whether he felt I would be well enough to attend. He was reassuring and urged me to focus on going; that said, there were three steps up to his office, and I was not even strong enough to climb them on my feet—I had to crawl up—and the course was only a month away.

Nevertheless, I was accepted, and I flew to London. I had forgotten how bone-chilling cold it can get in England, but when I stepped out from the airport on that drizzly November morning, I was aggressively reminded. Although I was certain that the mystery illness hadn't killed me, I felt the dampness might. Furthermore, I was there for four and a half weeks, and it rained—no, it poured, every day.

It was a wonderful course. We had top-notch lecturers and plenty of opportunities to be in the pool and hone our skills. My nine classmates were bright, supportive, and very funny. With all the work in the pool, I gradually became stronger, but I was not back to my full fitness for almost two years. Interestingly, once back home, I visited my doctor and told him I had attended the course.

He was very surprised. "Dear," he said gently, "I never thought you would get there. You were so sick, and I didn't want to say anything that might discourage you, as I was afraid it might make you worse."

The day I returned from the course, I sat at my desk, working at my typewriter, and Sally came skipping into the staff office. "Oh, Ruth," she said with great enthusiasm, "You're back!"

Sarcastically, I replied, "Yes, Sally, did you miss me?"

"Yes, Ruth," she said smiling impishly. "Things go much smoother when you are here." I almost fell off my chair but happily took it as a little olive branch.

Eventually, Vice-President Joan retired, but Manager Sally remained. The senior executives took the opportunity to restructure the organization, moving from five managers down to three, and so began a process of interviews to determine which two would go. Between my clinical work, committee work, and teaching, I knew all the managers very well, and so I was assigned to the selection board.

It was a huge learning experience. I had to read their resumes, which ran the spectrum from Sally's very concise, relevant, accurate summation on two pages to a great tome that may have been more valuable if weighed than read. In fact, one CV listed projects that the candidate described as initiated and chaired by her when, in truth, they were initiated and chaired by me. The nerve!

As we discussed the candidates afterwards, we could expound on more than just the resumes and interviews because we knew them so well. Unfortunately for Sally, some of the managers were very sweet people, but in a couple of cases, sugar was about the only substance. We all defended the ones we preferred and then left the executives to come to a decision.

I was having lunch downtown after having delivered my regular hydrotherapy lecture at the University of Toronto when I received a phone call that the management decisions had been made, and they were being shared with the selection board at that moment. Feeling quite certain that they were about to make the wrong choice, I rushed back to the hospital. Of course, they said they were going to let Sally go. I protested that, if they were sincere about a management structure for the purpose of moving the hospital forward with the best staff, then they couldn't release Sally. Yes, she needed to work on her interpersonal skills, but perhaps she could be offered advice on how to improve. I insisted that they couldn't deny that Sally was very bright, very skilled, well connected, and the best person to lead the hospital where we needed it to go. I didn't think we were looking for the most popular candidate but, rather, the best person for the job.

Well, it was certainly reluctantly, but they changed their minds, and Sally was one of the three successful candidates. Many of the staff were surprised, and others were disappointed.

Indeed, I had been hurt by her, but I had forgiven her and I could not, nor would I, deny that I had benefitted from her knowledge, skills, and practical efforts to help me continue my professional development. She gave me great confidence in my skills. I feel we owe it to each other to help improve our weaknesses, but we must be careful not to take the path of least resistance at the expense of overlooking the true value of someone's strengths. It's the old comparison of Hitler and Franklin Roosevelt—the former a clean living, non-smoker, and non-drinker, and the latter a smoker who died in his mistress's arms.

Not long after that, Sally was transferred to a position downtown and then fired. She was heartbroken, and I was saddened. I don't know whether she realized what a loyal friend she had in me once she got back out into the big bad world, but she started phoning, and she, Barbara, and I would go out to dinner four or five times per year. It was always a very jovial connection. She became a colleague/friend, a role she managed much better than being a boss. She was actually a lot of fun and usually up for anything.

In the autumn of 2011, I hadn't heard from her for a few months, so I called to see if she was okay. She informed me that she was not. She had undergone surgery for stage-four bowel cancer. She became very emotional when she asked me, "Ruth, will you pray for me?"

I felt enormous compassion. "Of course, Sally, I have been praying for you for years, and now I will just alter the focus."

I kept in regular contact with her over the next few weeks, but she was not doing well, despite her brave face. It was Christmas when I received a phone call from one of her friends, telling me that Sally was in the hospital. I went to the hospital, and she was delighted to see me. She thanked me for coming and said, "Oh Ruth, you must retire. You have paid your dues, and you don't owe the profession anything. I am so proud of you, especially for taking the hydrotherapy course and teaching. You are a very fine clinician."

I reminded her that I was too young to retire; however, my mother had been reciting the same mantra, and I promised them both that I would not work a day longer than I had to, and that would not be until the spring of 2015.

Before I left her room, I asked if I could pray with her. She hesitated briefly and then stretched out her hand and grasped mine. I thanked God for her and what she had meant to me as a clinical mentor. I assured her that I owed some of my success to her and that I was grateful.

Barbara and I visited her in palliative care at the beginning of February, only a few days before she finally stopped suffering on February 11, 2012.

CHAPTER 18

I had dated several different men in the first few years after coming home from England, but not any one person for very long. On one particular evening after having been out for dinner and the theatre, my date reached to kiss me and asked when he could see me again. It was such a simple thing, and yet I felt smothered and panicky.

"We'll talk," I said as I pulled away and went inside. Peach was in the kitchen cleaning the stovetop, although it was late—she was likely just occupying herself until I got home. I joined her in the kitchen, feeling compelled to have a heart to heart, and sat down at the table. "May I speak to you, Peach?"

"Yes, of course," she replied, carrying on at the stove.

"I realize that most mothers want their daughters to get married and have children, and I never want to disappoint you, but I can't do it. It just isn't in me."

Suddenly, Peach was sitting across from me, seemingly having floated from the stove to the table. Resting her chin in her hands, muffling her voice, she said, "Thank God!"

I was a little taken aback by her response, but said nothing.

"Ruthy, I am so relieved to hear you say that. I have always known that you were not the marrying kind, but I feared that you would get married due to social pressure and your religious beliefs, and I know you would not be happy. Ruthy, everyone was not born to be a doctor, a lawyer, or a teacher, and neither was everyone born to be a wife and mother. You must determine what you were born to be, and that is what you must be. Anything less than that will lead to a life of unhappiness, and no mother wants that for her children. Look at Marilyn. She has had a good education, a wonderful career, and has been free to travel the world, and there is a lot to be said for freedom. You were not born to be tied to a man and encumbered with children, and I have always known it, and I love you for the person you are. My only worry is that you are so cerebral that you will overlook your heart. Your mind is very powerful, but you can't just think your way through life."

"Peach, I promise I won't overlook my heart."

"Well, Ruthy, there is a lot to be said for friends, and you can certainly love your friends."

The next morning, she claimed she had had the best sleep in years.

"Why was that, Peach?"

"Because I went to bed with the peace of mind that you have finally recognized the Ruthy I know."

I like to think that I had kept my childhood promise to my parents. I was educated, had an excellent career, was making a respectable living, and ensured that they had everything they needed and wanted, although they didn't want much. I knew Dad quietly desired an interlocking brick walkway up to the veranda steps, and Peach always wished for siding on the house, as only the front was bricked. These were not inexpensive projects, but as I lived at home, I was able to save a good portion of my income and make their dreams come true. I helped myself by not being a careless spender. Furthermore, Marilyn advised me to put some money in Canada Savings Bonds, as they were getting a good interest rate at that time, and so I bought some every year and just kept rolling them over. I did pay rent every month, and I also took care of some medications Peach required that were not covered otherwise. Between everything, they were managing better than they'd ever done.

Marilyn had an aunt who owned and lived in a house that was very close to our church in Bloor West Village. I was still attending the same church and, in fact, was a deacon. Marilyn would occasionally comment on how her aunt's house would be perfect for me.

Facetiously, I would reply, "Sure, Marilyn, I can afford a house in that neighbourhood." I had been in it a few times, as Marilyn was a caregiver to her aunt, and I would accompany her when she attended to her duties from time to time. If one is the caregiver to an elderly person, it can be helpful to know a physiotherapist.

In January 1996, Aunt Winifred passed away, and Marilyn inherited the house. As the house was in a very desirable neighbourhood, several individuals approached Marilyn about purchasing it. Given the interest, Marilyn would have had no trouble selling it, but she wanted me to buy it. I didn't think I could afford it, so Marilyn arranged to get three real estate appraisals for the estate. I told her what I thought it was probably worth, and she offered what she thought it would fetch. We were tens of thousands apart, with me suggesting the higher amount.

I immediately made an appointment with my banker. As he knew me well (his wife was also a physiotherapist), it did not take long for him to outline how much mortgage I could carry and at what interest rate. He knew that I was famous for being a hard negotiator with the bank and assured me this was the best he could do. I still tried to haggle a bit but, knowing what the going rates were at the time, I left his office feeling that he had truly done his best. However, the most important thing was that I knew what I could offer Marilyn.

It was not long before the agents gave their evaluations. When Marilyn informed me of what they'd said, I reminded her that my estimate had been precisely the same; unfortunately, it was more than I had available to me. Marilyn asked what I could afford, but I was reluctant to tell her because it was exactly halfway between her estimate and the agents' estimate, a difference of a few thousand. I felt bad because I knew she wanted me to have the house, but this was her inheritance and, given the interest in the house before it was even on the market, she could have received quite a bit above the asking price. However, when I informed her of what my banker stated was my outside limit, she replied, coincidentally, that that was what she was asking. I could hardly believe it. She went on gently, "Ruth, sometimes good things should happen to good people."

The next thing I had to do was tell my parents, which was very difficult. I sat down alone with Peach first. I explained that Marilyn had offered me her aunt's house, and I would like to buy it. Then I started to cry.

"Why are you crying, Ruthy?"

"Because I don't know how you will manage without my money every month, and I can't afford both," I sobbed.

Patting me on the knee, she said, "Now you dry those tears. Remember what I have always told you: when fortune knocks upon your door, open it and let him in, or the next time, he will send his daughter, Miss Fortune!"

Of course, she made me laugh.

"Ruth, your father and I will manage. This is a wonderful opportunity for you, and you must not pass it up. I will not always be here, and it will be much easier for you if you are living independently before I die, rather than to try and deal with my death and learning to cope completely on your own all at the same time. Ruth, I have given you wings, and you must fly. Remember, when we love, we must hold close with an open hand. Now, you must go and tell your father."

I wasn't so concerned about Dad. I don't think I gave much thought to how he would react. He was a very agreeable chap, and my main worry was Peach. Nevertheless, I had to tell him, and so I simply said, "Dad, I am moving out. I am buying a house."

There was a very, very long silence. At first, I thought he hadn't heard me, but finally, he spoke. His tone was of a contemplative sadness: "It never occurred to me that you would ever leave us." That was all he ever said on the subject.

I moved in at the end of May 1996. My parents loved my house. It was built in 1925, and most of the original features remained, including leaded glass windows on either side of the fireplace. What Dad liked the best was the formal dining room. I would invite them over for a meal and to play cards on a Saturday evening. I would set the table with a cloth and silverware. Once seated, Dad would say, "My, my, isn't this lovely."

My dad never went out the door without proper attire, and that even included coming to my house. If he was only coming over to play cards, he would simply wear a jacket and tie, but if he was coming for dinner, he would wear a complete suit.

I suggested to Peach that she tell him that he was welcome to dress casually, but she said he wouldn't hear of it.

Laughing, I said, "Peach, when are you going to tell him that I am blind?"

"Ruth, you may be blind, but your father's respect for you supersedes that, and he would never do anything less for you than he would for anyone else."

Dad had no idea of my income and would not be able to fathom it if he did. He was always very concerned that I be able to pay my bills, so he would occasionally drop in with a bag of items that he bought while grocery shopping for him and Peach. He would show up with a big box of laundry powder, bathroom tissue, dishwashing liquid, or anything else he felt would help. I would thank him and try to gently let him know that he didn't need to bring me things, but Peach encouraged me to let him do so, as he like to feel supportive.

My parents were over for dinner one weekend after I had been in the house about six months. I served prime rib of beef, cabbage, sweet potatoes, and small roasted potatoes. It was the sort of traditional dinner my folks loved. We had a nice evening, and they left, seemingly happy. Once back at home, Dad sat in his chair with a long face and sighed. This was, for Peach, a clear indication that he was deeply troubled about something, so she asked what was wrong.

"Blanche, do you think Ruth is managing?"

"What do you mean, Lester? Look at that beautiful dinner she served us."

"Yes, Blanche, but all she had were those little tiny potatoes!"

When recounting the story to me later, Peach sighed, "You can take the boy out of the Bay, but you can't take the Bay out of the boy."

I just shook my head. "I guess, Peach, it isn't a potato until it is a great big tuber that one has to stand on the floor to peel."

When I was a child, I was always contemplating the future. I would mentally note where I was at any given moment so as not to forget young Ruth. It was as though I thought adult Ruth would be a different person and may need to be informed of the past to understand the present. One such very distinct moment was a Wednesday when I was ten years old. I was sitting cross-legged in the armchair with the wooden arms by the kitchen door, eating a banana. I thought, *My mother was thirty-seven when*

I was born, and so when I am thirty-seven, she will be twice my age. I wonder what I will be doing when I am thirty-seven and Peach is seventy-four.

I had been in my house less than a year when I turned thirty-seven. Peach, due to osteoarthritis, was scheduled to have a hip replacement. She and my father went for her pre-op assessment the day after my birthday. After work, I called to inquire how things had gone at the work-up, and she told me that the surgery was on hold and might not ever happen. I knew she wasn't joking by the tone in her voice, but my mind wasn't registering what was being said. She went on to say, "They took an X-ray of my lungs, standard procedure, they told me, and the doctor, a lovely woman, said that she saw a shadow that needed investigation. Consequently, my hip surgery was cancelled, and I was sent home to await the scheduling of some tests. Ruth, do you think I have cancer?"

My mind was spinning. No, not Peach. All I could think of was ten-year-old Ruth eating a banana and wondering what I would be doing on that day, and now I knew: praying for my beloved Peach.

So began a series of bloodwork, X-rays, CT scans, and lung biopsies. The first thing Peach was told before all the tests were completed or results were returned was that she'd had tuberculosis when she was younger.

"No," she said to the doctor. "I was in the tuberculosis sanatorium as a child, but that was because I was 'run down' and needed fresh eggs and milk, and my parents couldn't provide them."

The doctor didn't understand, but I did. Gently, I tried to explain it to her. "Peach, you were put in the sanatorium because you had tuberculosis, but they likely didn't tell you for fear that knowing your diagnosis might negatively impact your recovery. You believe in disclosure, Peach, but that is not how people used to think in those days and, rightly or wrongly, they thought they were helping you."

Peach had always adored her mother, but now she felt enormously hurt and betrayed. Fighting tears, she said, "To think they allowed me to live a lie all these years."

I had Peach stay overnight with me the day before getting the results of the biopsy. As we sat together, Peach rocking by the fireplace, we discussed all the possibilities of the doctor's visit.

"Ruth," she said encouragingly, "if this is cancer, we will deal with it. And, if it is not, we will rejoice. But, honey, either way, God loves us, and it doesn't get any better than that!"

As we entered the doctor's examination room, it was as though time stood still. The bustle of the hospital outside the door disappeared as we sat in a sort of vacuum devoid of everything except nervous energy that was grasping embarrassingly to a thin thread of hope. The respirologist sat before us, rustling the pages of Peach's file. "Mrs. Vallis, you don't have cancer."

I don't think Peach heard anything else he said. She just sat there in an almost deflated relief. He did say that she had an idiopathic reactive epithelial tissue that they would monitor. She thanked God and then thanked the doctor. A few weeks later, she had her hip replaced, and she went back to enjoying life enthusiastically.

CHAPTER 19

Living in Bloor West Village was the perfect situation for me. Marilyn was right. I could walk to the subway, bank, shopping, restaurants, theatre, and church, among other things, which was essential for someone who would never be able to drive. However, Bloor Street could get very busy with people, fruit stands, tables outside cafés, and car drivers and pedestrians who were often not paying attention. One day, as I was walking home from work, an older woman, apparently window shopping, tripped over my white cane and fell. She was not seriously hurt, but I was mortified. It was that moment that I determined that now that I was living in my own house, I would apply for a guide dog.

There are a number of guide dog schools—a few in Canada and several in the United States. I had heard bits and pieces about all of them, but the one that seemed to best fit my needs was the Guide Dog Foundation for the Blind in Long Island, New York. The application process was lengthy and involved. By August of 1998, all my requirements were fulfilled, and all that was left for me to do was wait, and wait, and wait. It often takes a long time to get one's first dog and, for me, the wait was fourteen months.

I explained to my parents that I had applied for a guide dog. I think it is accurate to say they were not delighted. They reminded me that they felt it was a life of confinement and slavery for the dog, and they would always be feeling sorry for the animal. Be that as it may, I assured them I would be going to New York on October 10, Canadian Thanksgiving weekend, to receive and train with my new dog. Marilyn dropped me off at the airport with the instructions to bring home a beautiful companion. Both Marilyn and my colleague Barbara were great dog lovers and, contrary to my parents' opinions, thought that my getting a guide dog was a wonderful idea.

It was Tuesday afternoon when they brought her to me. She was a fifteen-and-a-half-month-old black lab named Sophie. I will admit I was a little afraid, as I was not used to dogs. Most of my ten classmates had previous guide dogs, so they were excited to meet their new companions, but I was just nervous.

Each person waited alone in their room where their dog was brought for a private meet and greet. My instructor, Barbara Kaiser, came in, handed me a leash, and said, "This is Sophie." With that, Sophie just lay down at my feet. I could hear the others in their rooms with their dogs excitedly bouncing around, barking, nails clicking on the linoleum, and happy handlers saying, "Hi, buddy." Sophie just lay there. I stroked her velvet ears and then felt around to find an on-switch someone had forgotten to engage. Nothing, just a big, smooth dog lying on the floor, either contented or unconscious, and I wasn't certain which one. *Perhaps she doesn't like me,* I wondered, *and this is resignation?* My parents are going to say they told me so.

For the most part, the training went well. I became more comfortable with her as a guide and a friend. She was very obedient. I had only to call her name once, and she would immediately be at my side. She was calm and quiet, and she never barked. The others in the class would tease me, calling her Lady Sophie and ask what time she would be serving tea, and would she be wearing white gloves while sticking out her pinky? However, while walking outdoors one morning, Sophie began to limp. The instructors immediately stopped us and examined her paw to see if she had picked up a stone or cut her pad. They saw nothing, and we continued. Later that afternoon, while walking indoors, Sophie suddenly sat down and turned her head to favour her left hind leg. Concerned that something must be wrong, instructor Barbara took her in to see the Guide Dog Foundation vet. Her paws were examined, and her hips were X-rayed with no evidence of any injury or anything else that might explain the intermittent limping. The other students were very worried for me and Sophie. There is great heartache if someone's dog has to be taken away after training has begun, as the bonding has also begun. However, Lady Sophie was returned to me, and we continued with the training and the teasing.

I enjoyed my classmates, but I was glad to get home where the real test of my training would be revealed. It is one thing to be walking with a guide dog with a sighted instructor watching from even a long way off, but it is quite another thing to venture out on one's own with a dog. It takes some effort to put one's trust in four paws and a wagging tail; however, needs must.

In order to teach the dog one's neighbourhood and the places one frequents, one goes to the door of a shop, restaurant, etc., tells the dog the name of the place, turns around, and walks a few steps away and then asks the dog to find the place you have named. If she does, she is praised, the door handle is tapped, and the name is reinforced.

After being in New York for a month, I needed to go to the bank. Fortunately, the bank was right on the corner, so it would be easy to find. I gave Sophie all the correct instructions to find the door, and she did. I tapped the door handle and said, "Bank. Good, bank." We turned and walked several steps away and then turned around again. I instructed her to find the bank. She took me straight to the door. Excited about her first success, I praised her vigorously. I then opened the door and, upon entering, repeated, "Bank. Good, bank," and she must have agreed, as she left a deposit of her own.

Sophie quickly became a very popular part of my life. She was smart, obedient, sensitive, and gentle. Yes, you guessed it, my parents fell in love with her. They were pleased with the way I treated her and the way she responded. Peach was particularly enamored. If we were walking along the street and Peach was lagging behind, Sophie would look back to ensure she was with us and, if not, Sophie would stop and wait for her to catch up. My folks admitted they felt much more comfortable about me living alone and travelling back and forth to work, knowing that Sophie was always with me.

A big problem we have in Toronto in the winter is all the salt that is poured out on the roads and sidewalks to prevent ice. It is nasty stuff, especially on dog paws. Sophie was in obvious distress whenever walking in it.

Consequently, I bought boots for her, which she hated. I tried to get her used to them by putting them on her in the house. She would collapse on the floor with all her legs splayed out in every direction. I would instruct her to stand up, but she assured me that she could not possibly stand up in boots. I tried lifting her, but once I let go, she landed on her stomach all flattened out again. It was as though she were made of jelly. I never liked to use treats as a form of encouragement or tool of praise, but she was a lab, and the way to her heart was definitely through her stomach. With Sophie still lying completely flat on the floor and with boots in situ, I went into the kitchen and opened a box of biscuits. Suddenly, she leaped to her paws and came bounding to me with her leather-soled boots slapping on the ceramic tile floor, sounding like a race horse galloping to the finish line. Of course, it was my mistake: she couldn't walk in the boots, but she could run in them. I became tired of battling with her to put them on, so I tried different kinds of protective salves for her pads that were expensive, messy, and never worked. Finally, I just gave up.

This reminded me of myself as a child. Peach and I often walked to the local shopping centre on a Saturday morning. I distinctly recall one day in early December when I was about twelve. Peach and I headed out together. I, a fairly normal almost-teenager, was without gloves. I don't know why children don't like to dress properly in cold weather, but I was guilty of frequently not wearing gloves or mittens. Peach noticed my bare hands and asked me if I had any gloves. I said no and denied feeling uncomfortable. My hands were getting numb and likely pretty red. A few minutes later, Peach stopped, opened her handbag and withdrew a pair of my mittens.

"Why don't you put these on, honey?" she encouraged. I must admit it was a huge improvement. "Does that feel better?"

"Yes," I admitted sheepishly.

With that, she wrapped an arm around me and said cheerfully, "I love you."

Years later, when I asked her about having a pair of my mittens in her handbag, she laughed and explained that she knew I would likely go out without my gloves, and so she packed a pair for me. "You see, Ruth, a good parent has to be just a little bit smarter than their children. There would have been no benefit in me chastising you or punishing you for not wearing gloves by letting you get frostbitten hands. There was more to be learned by teaching you the benefits of dressing warmly."

One very cold winter day, Sophie and I headed for the bus that we caught at the subway. Sophie was hopping on three paws and crying, which made me feel terrible, but I had tried everything. The bus was waiting when we arrived. I greeted the driver, who got up and left the vehicle as soon as I sat down. He appeared again a few minutes later with a wad of paper towels soaked in hot water. He got down and washed the salt off Sophie's paws. He then grabbed a stack of clean towels and dried her. I then produced her boots out of my knapsack and, together, we put them on her. She didn't fight us but, instead, leaned against me with her head resting in my lap. I stroked her ears and assured her that I loved her. She seemed to understand just as I had understood Peach with the mittens.

I asked the driver what made him think to go get the towels. He said we were late, which never happened, and so he had waited for a couple of minutes. When he saw us, he realized that Sophie was suffering and why. I was so grateful and touched by his kindness. Sophie and I sent a letter to the Toronto Transit Commission, informing them of what Daniel had done and asked them to recognize his thoughtfulness, which they did.

As the name suggests, Hillcrest Hospital was perched on top a hill at a very busy intersection. We often took one bus and then walked the ten minutes up Bathurst Street to the steep hill of Austin Terrace and around to the hospital driveway. In the winter, we would often take a bus up Bathurst to avoid some of the salt and treacherous footing. Austin Terrace was situated between two stops, but bus drivers would often ask if I was going to the hospital and drop me right at the corner.

One hot July Monday in 2000, I decided to take the Bathurst bus for Sophie's sake. The driver kindly dropped us off just south of the corner of Austin Terrace. Traffic was very heavy, so as soon as we disembarked, he pulled away. Once Sophie and I rounded the corner and headed up the steep hill, I heard a woman moan as though in great pain. Then I realized the moan had come from me, although it sounded distinctly separate. I had fallen into a ditch. There was a house at the corner undergoing major landscaping, which I did not know, and apparently, vandals had destroyed the flimsy barricade that had been erected around the ditch. A high brick retainer wall on Bathurst prevented anyone from seeing it until they were around the corner. I managed to hold on to Sophie's leash, but she wasn't going anywhere anyway. She lay on the pavement slightly above me and quivered. I was soon spotted by a passerby and taken to hospital where several injuries were identified, but I was able to go home and receive treatment on an out-patient basis.

Marilyn was also going through a difficult period at the time with the loss of her own dog and a colleague/friend. My accident was probably the last straw for her emotionally, as she did something she had never done before. She walked in her sleep. That might not seem like much, except that she stepped out into space at the top of a flight of stairs. Waking mid tumble, she realized she was falling, but could do nothing to stop it. The momentum was broken by the newel post, which she destroyed. However, it was better that than destroying herself on the marble tile floor that met her at the bottom. She sustained a small fracture in her neck and wrist, with multiple deep bruises, but fortunately, she had no spinal cord or brain injury—or worse.

After a few weeks of therapy and recovery, I felt well enough to return to work. We took the bus and then walked up Bathurst. As we approached the corner, Sophie slowed down. I urged her forward, but once we got to the place where the ditch had been, she stopped completely. "It's okay, Sophie. Forward," I instructed, but she only stood, trembling, and vomited.

Meanwhile, the landscaping company and homeowners blamed Sophie, suggesting that she was not a good guide dog. Sophie, of course, felt completely responsible and grieved over what had happened. From then on, we always approached the hospital driveway from a different direction. It was causing her too much anxiety even months later.

Dogs are so loyal and forgiving that it is not hard to love them. However, it never ceases to amaze me just how much they are loved and to what lengths people will go for them. One morning, all the physiotherapists were walking down the corridor to the treatment area after a meeting when we were met with an overwhelming stench of diarrhea. The complaints started to fly. "Who would send a patient to therapy like that? I hope it isn't one of mine, as I am not in the mood to clean that up first thing in the day!" And on it went. As we passed my office, I opened the door to fetch something before going to the gym. Surprise! It wasn't a patient. Sophie had had an explosive bowel movement that had sprayed the door, the walls, the floor, everything. Once the staff realized that Sophie was the one in trouble, they all came running. Someone took her outside while one chap grabbed a bucket and cloths and went to work on cleaning my office. There was an enormous outpouring of compassion, a 180-degree shift of emotion from when they thought a patient was the culprit.

I don't know whether the involuntary bowel movement was a symptom of greater problems, but I suspect it was. The occasional limping returned. She would also scream out in the night and, initially, I wasn't certain whether she was having bad dreams or was in pain. Nevertheless, I took her back to our vet. The joints of her hind legs were poked, prodded, and stressed, and they found no evidence of anything wrong. So I took her home and tried to convince myself that I had imagined something bigger than it was. However, the night crying, limping, and occasional day crying continued. Back to the vet we went. There were several doctors at the clinic, and they all had a look at her, with her primary vet always part of the assessment for continuity. No one could identify or diagnose anything. I was starting to be treated like a neurotic new mother. Admittedly, I didn't know much about dogs in general, but I lived with Sophie twenty-four seven and had been a physiotherapist for fifteen years, and I could not imagine that all dogs limped, cried, and vomited.

I was starting to wonder whether guiding was too stressful for her when one morning, we left the locker room at work and headed up the stairs to my office. Sophie hesitated, but when I urged her up, she struggled to climb the stairs, and I had to help her. This could be ignored no longer. I called the vet and took her in that day. I was firm with the doctor when I suggested that there was no point in examining her again. "She needs to be seen by a specialist," I insisted. An appointment was made with a canine orthopaedic surgeon in Mississauga.

The surgeon's clinic was a forty-five-minute drive from my house, so my colleague Barbara offered to take us there. I was grateful for her help, as she lived in Mississauga and, therefore, knew the area. She was also a dog owner and physiotherapist, and I felt more comfortable, and perhaps legitimate, having her beside me.

Barbara and I sat together while the surgeon pushed, pulled, and pressed hard all over Sophie's hind legs without being able to elicit any reaction. One of the blessings of labs is that they are so cooperative and agreeable, but it is also one of their downfalls. They would rather suck it up than admit to anything that might not please their master.

When the surgeon said, "I can't find anything wrong," I lost it.

"Darn you, doctor," I snapped, smacking the arm of my chair. "You may be a good orthopaedic surgeon, but I am a good physiotherapist, and there is something wrong with that dog. Doctor," I snarled, "examine her spine. Everyone keeps looking at her hips and legs, and I believe the intermittent nature of her symptoms indicates something more neurological than musculoskeletal."

"She has a very well-defined musculature," he pointed out.

"That may be so, but then you explain the limping, crying, vomiting, and involuntary bowel movements."

He agreed to keep her overnight, run some tests in the morning, and call me in the afternoon. As we got up to leave, he assured me that they would take good care of her, saying she would have ground beef and rice for dinner and a nice bed to sleep in. I found the last comment a patronizing attempt at assurance to the neurotic new mother.

It was barely afternoon, twelve exactly, when my office phone rang. I was surprised to hear the surgeon's voice so soon. "I have X-rayed Sophie's spine."

All I could think was, *is that all?* What I said was, "And, doctor?"

"I am concerned," he replied. My body stiffened. I have been in health care a long time, and if you admit to being concerned, then there is something very wrong.

"What did you find?"

"Well, Ruth, as you know, humans have five lumbar vertebrae, but dogs have seven. Sophie's seventh lumbar vertebrae is overgrown and compressing her terminal spinal cord."

My heart sank, but at the same time, I felt angrily vindicated. The veterinarian told me there was an American veterinary neurosurgeon in Mississauga, and he would make an appointment for Sophie with him.

The one thing I learned through all of this was the difference between human and veterinary medicine. Three days later, February 1, 2001, Sophie was at her appointment. The neurosurgeon explained that this tended to happen more often in large breed dogs such as St. Bernards. The classic sign was the dog's inability to stand on her hind legs. Well, of course, the only indication I had of anything like that was her recent problem climbing stairs. He took her front paws and tried to stand her upright, and she screamed! She was on the operating table the next day.

The surgery was long and expensive, but as Sophie was a very young dog and the symptoms had begun while we were still in class, the Guide Dog Foundation negotiated a fee with the surgeon, and they covered it. Barbara and I went to pick her up. She seemed pleased to see us, although in pain. We were instructed to lift her into the car. She weighed sixty-eight pounds, and we were not to move her spine. It was a difficult task, but nothing is impossible for two seasoned physios, or that is what we liked to believe. She was not allowed to climb stairs or curbs for six weeks, so I had a carpenter build ramps into my house. She wasn't allowed any pain medication, as they didn't want her to move too much. As my bedroom was upstairs, I slept on the living room floor beside her every night to comfort and reassure her. However, I had to go to work, so I arranged with my former vice-president to come in during the day to take her out. Joan would kindly bring things to read or do and just spend time at my house so the days would not be so long for Sophie.

Unfortunately, the pain made her chew. I didn't mind it when it was her bed and toys, but when I came home to find an arm missing from an armchair, I was a little less than pleased! The bills from all the visits were mounting, and I hadn't budgeted for new furniture.

Eventually, Sophie started to work again. She appeared pleased to be back in a harness but moved very slowly. Everyone was glad to see her out and about, and she enjoyed the attention. However, it was not long before the night screams started again, and she was soon crying out in the day as well, sometimes even when just lying still and doing nothing.

In April, we travelled to Rochester, New York, where a classmate, Christine Dandrea, and her family were hosting a big fundraiser for the Guide Dog Foundation. I was asked to speak on my experience with a guide dog. My instructor, Barb, was there, and as we entered the hall, Barb asked me to continue while she stopped to look at something. I don't think she wanted to, but she had to admit that she'd noticed Sophie was limping. My heart sank, but I steeled myself for the evening while, in the back of my mind, I knew there would be another visit to the vet in the very near future.

Everyone was quiet when we walked into the clinic, not wanting to think that Sophie was not doing well. Unfortunately, the neurosurgeon had returned to the US, so we were sent, instead, to a veterinary neurologist. Her office was in the east end of the city, but she was worth the trip. She was a kind and compassionate woman who knew dogs well but also understood the important safety factor that a working dog provided for a blind handler. She was struck by the innately obedient nature of Sophie. When X-raying a spine and hips, the dog is usually given an anaesthetic, as they are placed on their back with their hind legs positioned like a frog. Sophie never required an anaesthetic for this procedure, as she would lie on her back, hold her legs in the way instructed, and not move until told to do so.

Sadly, the X-rays revealed that the lumbar spine was overgrowing again. It was not what I wanted to hear. Furthermore, I noticed that Sophie was not holding her head up as high as previously. This may have been a result of the scar tissue around her nerves and spinal cord from the surgery, or it may have indicated that the cervical spine in her neck was also overgrowing.

There are those things in life that one knows in one's heart but does not want to admit openly, and certainly what the doctor was about to say was already running in the back of my mind.

"Ruth," she said gently, "it is time to stop Sophie's suffering."

"Doctor," I wailed, "you are talking about my baby."

"Yes, I know, but she is suffering."

"I know she is suffering," I sobbed, "and I am suffering with her. I am the one who noticed the problem. I am the one who insisted to all the so-called professionals that something was wrong when no one believed me. I had construction done to my house. I slept on the floor beside her for weeks. I investigated acupuncture and other alternative medicines. She chewed my furniture. I have spent a fortune, and now what? This? It is not that I resent any of it, but is there nothing else?"

Softly, the doctor offered, "I can take her home for a week and observe her to see if we have missed something, but I think it will result in the same outcome."

"No," I whispered, feeling beaten. "I will take her home and call her vet."

The neurologist must have gone right to the phone, as our doctor was waiting to hear from me. She suggested that under the circumstances, it might be better for Sophie to die in her own home. We scheduled a date for ten days hence. I felt sick and disloyal. Of course, I was doing it for her sake, but I couldn't explain it to her, and she would just go on being sweet and loving while I had made an appointment for her death. In the midst of it all, a long-time colleague said that I had changed since getting Sophie. She said that I had revealed a tenderness she had never seen in me before. Perhaps it would have been easier to have overlooked my heart, but it wasn't possible.

I know my parents were grieving for Sophie, but they were also grieving for me. They knew it was the right decision, but they couldn't make it for me. They could only stand by and watch me struggle. Peach came to visit me, likely to see Sophie again, but also to offer words of comfort. She told me that she felt that when people, and very possibly animals, had prolonged and painful ends to their lives, they gave the ones they loved a signal that it was time, and right, to let go. "I believe that Sophie will let you know that you are doing the right thing." I appreciated Peach's attempt to soothe my aching heart, but I couldn't imagine how Sophie would communicate any such thing to me.

Three days before the appointment, I had to run an errand. I reached for Sophie's leash and harness and called her to me. Silence. I called her again. Silence. I knew she was in the general vicinity, and my heart started to race, as she had never needed to be called more than once before this.

"Sophie, come please."

Slowly, she moved toward me and leaned her entire weight against my legs.

"We need to go out," I said as I raised the harness toward her head. With that, she dropped her nose to the floor and leaned in even harder as if to say, *Please don't make me guide. I just can't do it anymore.* The message was loud and clear. Peach was right.

May 18, 2001, was a drizzly day. It was as though even the heavens were crying. Marilyn wanted to be with me, and I agreed, although I wanted to be alone. I sat on the floor and held Sophie as the vet administered the massive dose of anaesthetic. It was not long before the doctor whispered, "She's gone."

The thing that struck me most, and I remember most distinctly, is that Sophie was a very warm dog with a very cold nose, and within seconds, she became a very cold dog with a very warm nose. Furthermore, I had been warned that she might empty her bowels and bladder, but she did not. She was too much of a lady for that—Lady Sophie to the very end. I suppose the most striking thing about all of it is that there is nothing on earth as final as death, and there is a hollowness that makes it so difficult to be the one who is left behind.

It was not long before I received a call from the vet that Sophie's ashes were ready for me to pick them up. Marilyn had offered to go with me, but I wanted to be alone. I walked in, said her name, and was handed a small paper shopping bag. I paid the $324.25 and left. It was a beautiful, warm spring day, and everyone in Bloor West Village seemed to be out. As I tapped carefully along, I was so aware of the voices talking and laughing. I couldn't understand why everyone sounded so happy and carefree while I felt as though I was barely moving through a vacuum. Somehow, there was one world out there and a completely different world inside of me that was crumbling down. At home, I opened the bag and found a box. Inside the box was tissue paper. Inside the tissue paper was a textured, hand-painted oval pottery urn. Inside the urn was a plastic bag of ashes, all carefully tied with a ribbon. I wrapped the urn in the tissue paper, placed it in the box, tucked it into the bag, and stashed it on a shelf in my bedroom closet. I didn't want anyone to see it, and yet I didn't know what else to do with it. I knew I didn't want to bury it in the back garden just in case I ever moved, but that was a decision for another day.

Two weeks later, it was Communion Sunday at church and, as a deacon, I was responsible for offering a prayer of thanks for the cup. I had done it many times before, but suddenly, with my heart still raw, the truth of what we were celebrating and why was revealed to me like never before. As Peach said to me, "When one loves, one must hold close with an open hand." Here, I had been struggling with some vain, shallow excuse for love that was preventing me from making a decision to put Sophie out of her suffering for no one's sake but her own. Now, I was standing before the Communion table, set with bread and wine, the symbol of the ultimate expression of love. God purposely sent His only Son into the world to die for us. Jesus was not released from His suffering for His sake, but rather, made to suffer for mine. How much love would it take to send one's own perfect Son into an unworthy world and sacrifice that Son to save sinners from themselves? It is unfathomable. I wept through that prayer, so aware of the great difference between God's love and mine.

I was back to getting around with a white cane and everyone noticed. "Where is your dog?" I was asked on the street, in the restaurants and shops, and on the public transit. I answered that question approximately three hundred times and then, of course, there was everyone at work. They had come to love Sophie, and their grief was palpable. Some staff couldn't even speak to me because they were so broken up.

One morning, as the Bathurst bus doors opened, the driver yelled out, "No one is allowed on this bus without a beautiful guide dog." As I stepped aboard, I explained why I was using my cane. The full-to-overflowing vehicle went silent. The driver choked out an apology and then sat for a few moments, composing himself before driving again. At the next stop, most of the passengers disembarked and patted my shoulder or offered words of condolence while sniffling.

Peach asked if I was going to get another dog, but I didn't think I could go through that again. "Well, it may not be anything like this the next time, Ruth."

"That's a funny question from you, Peach, after all your opposition."

"I know, but your father and I can't imagine you without a dog now."

When I called the Foundation to inquire about another dog, my instructors, Barb and Kim, who had been so supportive through every-thing, seemed pleased that I was considering returning to the school.

CHAPTER 20

It was August 27, 2001, when I received the phone call from Barb informing me that they had a dog that they believed would be a good fit for me. Part of me was relieved, while another voice in me screamed, *No, there is only one dog for me, and she is a pile of ashes tied with a ribbon in a plastic bag, in a pottery urn, in tissue paper, in a box, in a paper bag, and on a shelf in my closet.* Barb explained that I would be flown to New York on September 23, and class would start the next day. Fighting tears, I thanked her and assured her that I would arrange with the hospital to have time off.

I had a fun and motivated caseload of patients at the time. The nine o'clock appointments were all there early and working hard on that fateful Tuesday morning. Knowing that I was preparing to get a new dog, they were asking me questions about guide dogs, and I was entertaining them with exaggerated stories of putting one's trust in an unsuspecting creature. As always, there was plenty of laughter, but suddenly, it all went quiet. As usual, I had the radio on, softly giving out news, traffic reports, and weather forecasts. Although the volume had not been increased, it seemed to blare into everyone's consciousness. A plane, and then a second plane, had flown into the World Trade Center in New York. All activity in the hospital came to a halt as staff and patients alike gathered around radios and televisions listening for the latest updates. Although the Guide Dog Foundation was on Long Island, there was much concern because no one knew how far-reaching the attacks might extend or for how long. Needless to say, none of the patients were interested in physiotherapy treatment for the rest of that day, so a group of us physios, wanting to do something, went to donate blood.

We were not the only people with that idea. The Toronto Film Festival was on, but it was now dark due to the circumstances, and so many of the young festival volunteers had also lined up to donate. A local restaurant sent over boxes of pizza to feed those in the long queue. It was as though everyone wanted to help each other be prepared to help the rest if needed.

The Americans, while grieving mightily, were trying to show the world that they would not be intimidated. It was, as much as possible, business as usual. Word was that the guide dog class was going forward. Initially, that presented a problem for me. The airports were closed, and I had no way of getting there. My pastor at the time, David Emery, and his wife, Sue, loved Sophie, but they were very encouraging and in complete agreement with me returning for a new dog. Pastor David suggested that if the planes did not start flying in time, he would drive me down and pick me up after if necessary. I hoped it would not be necessary, but it was a very generous offer.

Peach asked me to reconsider. "It is not safe, honey, and I hate to think of you there during such uncertain times."

"Peach, I have to go. My baby dog is waiting for me, and I can't leave her there with danger looming and breathing those fumes from the crumbled buildings."

"Well, when you put it like that, I guess you are right. Go and get your little girl and come home safe and sound."

The planes started flying again just a few days ahead of my scheduled flight. They say it is an ill wind that blows no good, and that is how I felt about the airport. It was a ghost town that Sunday morning. No line-ups, no luggage to trip over, and plenty of attention from the staff. However, I have often been a magnet for odd people, and that day was no exception. There was a woman in the waiting area who was screaming and crying and having a major panic attack. Of course, she came and sat beside me. I did my best to calm her, assuring her that my church was praying for me, and that if she was on my flight, she would likely be okay.

Fortunately, although the plane was not full, her seat was several rows behind me, making it a fairly comfortable journey. Once on the ground at

LaGuardia airport, she came up to me and thanked me for helping her get through the flight. One might ask why someone would fly if they were so frightened. She had a good reason: she was going to visit friends for Rosh Hashanah. I certainly understood her for, undoubtedly, more than ever, the world needed to celebrate a new day, a new year, and a new hope.

On Tuesday afternoon, all the students gathered to receive the long-awaited news—the gender, breed, and name of their dog.

"Ruth: female, golden retriever. Name: Ruby."

What? A golden retriever? *No, my dog is black!* screamed my brain. I didn't hear anything else about any other dog. I just sat in shock. We were sent to our rooms to await our new guides. I sat on my bed, fighting tears. Sophie was gone. I had made the decision to get a new dog, and I had to give her a chance, but a golden retriever named Ruby? After a few brief minutes, I heard Barb speaking softly to a dog who sounded like she was prancing down the hall. She stopped obediently at the door and waited until she was instructed inside. She came directly to me. Barb handed me the leash and quietly disappeared. Ruby promptly sat up on her haunches, back ramrod straight, front toes gently touching my knees for balance, and looked straight into my face as if to say, *You'll do!* She was fluffy and soft. Suddenly, she stood up on her hind legs as if to say, *See? I can do it. My spine is fine.*

On the third day of training, while Ruby and I marched along in Kings Park with Barb at our side, I stated that I had developed a cardiac condition.

"No," Barb exclaimed. "What happened?"

"I have little golden paw prints on my heart."

Barb squeezed my arm, and I could sense her broadening smile.

Matching a handler with a guide dog is a little science and a whole lot of art. The Foundation staff make a concerted effort to get the right fit, but I have never quite understood how they decided that both Sophie and Ruby were right for me. If Sophie was a sophisticated lady, Ruby was a diva. Sophie had a slow and steady gait and was always sensitive to and concerned about others. Ruby marched along at a determined pace and, if you couldn't keep up, that was your problem.

People would often comment on Ruby's expressive face. Apparently, she would raise one eyebrow, then the other, then wrinkle her brows.

The young staff in training used to laugh and say that we were like a Fido advert where the dog and person looked alike. They said that every time she looked at me, she had an expression of, *I wuv you.* However, if she caught people looking at her, her face said, *Who do you think you're looking at!?* This was corroborated by a Jamaican nurse at my hospital who suggested, sucking her teeth, "If I couldn't see that dog's blonde coat, I would say she was a West Indian teenager—what an attitude!"

There were two issues with Ruby with which we worked hard to try and correct. She had terrible separation anxiety. It didn't matter whether I went out for five minutes or two hours. There was always the same reaction. Ruby would be right at the door, hopping up and down on her hind legs, grabbing my clothing in her teeth, and squealing at the top of her lungs. I tried many well-recognized techniques with direction from the Foundation and other dog experts, but they just didn't work with the diva. Neighbours would inform me that whenever I went out without her, there would be a golden face pressed against the window, anxiously peering out the entire time.

On one occasion, I returned home after being out for an hour. There was no one there to greet me at the door. I felt a momentary sense of relief and concern all mixed up together. Then I heard a sound upstairs and thought, *Wow, maybe we have made some headway.* Perhaps she'd just gone up to her bed and waited there. She was waiting, all right. She had dragged my duvet off my bed and piled it in her bed. She'd then put my pillows on top and was jumping up and down on the very top of the massive mound of bedding while squealing. I think she was singing, "I'm the queen of the castle;" however, I disagreed and informed her that, more likely, she was the dirty rascal. I surrendered. She was a very smart and willing dog and, obviously, the separation anxiety was causing her to suffer, and she didn't deserve that. From that day on, she went everywhere with me and was delighted to do so.

The other issue was barking. It wasn't so bad when we were at home, but it was an uncomfortable situation for me at the hospital. If someone came into my office when I wasn't there, she would say nothing, but if someone came in when I was there, she would say plenty. Now, mind you, sometimes it came in handy.

I had to work one Saturday, and as it was an early weekend morning, there was no one else around at the subway where we waited for the bus. Apparently, there was a bus parked over from me, but because the motor wasn't running, I was not aware. Ruby was sitting patiently by my side. Suddenly and slowly, she stood up and put herself across in front of me, peering back over her shoulder. Unbeknownst to me, there was a man quietly sneaking toward me. As he came close, Ruby spun around, faced him, growling and barking. He jumped back. Stammering out his justification for his approach, he asked for the time and left. With that, a bus driver appeared from the stationary vehicle. "If you were my wife or daughter, I would give that dog a bone."

"No, she's not supposed to bark."

"Oh no, you didn't see that character. He was up to no good, and she knew it and said so. She is a great dog, and you let her bark." Unfortunately, it wasn't that simple. Barking at a possible mugger is one thing, but barking at a patient is another.

Again, we tried everything. Finally, we invested in an expensive citronella collar. I would never use a shock collar on a dog, but I was willing to try this. It was a lightweight nylon collar with a small cube that rested against her voice box. When she barked, the cube would release a mist of citronella oil, a lemon-like substance that is supposed to be repulsive to dogs. The theory was that they would bark, the lemon would spray up, and the dog would hate it and stop barking. It was a great theory; however, the Canadians who invented it never met Diva Ruby. You see, she thought it was perfume. She drove me crazy with her bark, spray, sniff, bark, spray, sniff. She would then look around as though to say, *I smell pretty, don't you think?* I am sure she would have preferred Chanel No. 5, but she settled for citronella. I surrendered again. There were several battles I did win, but I came to terms with those things that were not likely to change.

Besides having to deal with the very smart and challenging Miss Ruby, a.k.a. Velcro, I was also having to face some significant changes in the world of physiotherapy and health care. I think the twenty-first century has been the century of competition. Businesses and organizations want to say that they have recruited the top 10 or 20 percent of employees, and the only way to evidence these things is on paper. Consequently, there is an increasing demand for degrees and certificates, which is no more than a statement that an individual has completed a course, not a reflection of competence or creativity.

I was lecturing to and coordinating physiotherapy students who were earning master's degrees. Furthermore, discussions had begun about making it a doctoral program. Meanwhile, I was feeling the pressure. I had a physiotherapy qualification and an accredited certificate in hydrotherapy, but I did not want management to have an excuse to say I was no longer fit for the job. I was keeping up with my knowledge and skills, but if another piece of paper would bring about a little more job security, I would have to get one.

I had been friends with a physio colleague from Hillcrest, Fidelma Serediuk, and although our careers took us in different directions, we kept in touch, going out for dinner or to the art gallery every so often. In fact, let me digress and say Fidelma is gifted in making visual art palpable through verbal description.

We were at the Art Gallery of Ontario, home of Claes Oldenburg's Floor Burger, at an exhibit of Rubens. I was wearing a headset that was providing name and historical significance of each piece. However, Fidelma was adding her perspective as well. As we approached one of Rubens's signature voluptuous women, Fidelma gasped and whispered, "Oh, she looks as though if one were to fall against her, one would sink into her flesh!" What a beautiful image.

I confided in Fidelma my fears of being left behind as the younger clinicians were getting more and more qualifications. She was struggling with the same concerns, and she invited me to meet for dinner and talk about it. In the meantime, I searched available programs at all the universities in Toronto, as it didn't occur to me to look any farther afield.

Fidelma, too, had been searching for appropriate courses and, apparently, there were dozens available all over the world, including some that offered distance learning, which was necessary because the overseas quarantine regulations would not permit me to take Ruby, and she would have never allowed me to go without her even if I had wanted to. Over dinner, Fidelma told me, dropping her voice as though to share a great secret, that the University of Greenwich in London, England, offered a master's of science degree in Continuing Professional Development Health—completely online. I could study from home without any disruption to Ruby or the hassle of having to navigate a new campus. I left the restaurant feeling a little excited, although I knew I had some serious thinking to do.

My New Year's resolution for 2002 was to apply for that master's program. I completed the application and wrote my letter of intent, but I did not send it immediately, as I wanted a little more time to think and pray about it first. It would be a three-year commitment, and I would still be working full-time.

It has often been said that life is what happens when one is planning something else and, of course, my life has been no exception. We were enjoying a beautiful late-January thaw. My good friend and walking companion Carol Swanston and I were taking advantage of the warm day and were on a jaunt around the hospital neighbourhood over the lunch hour. I had a very busy afternoon planned, with a pool therapy session at one and the assessment of two new patients after that.

Back at work, Barbara arrived to read the new charts to me. We were just into the first chart when I received a page indicating an outside call. The voice at the other end identified himself as a police officer. He asked if Lester Vallis was my father. I said yes.

"Your father died today," he stated in a rather matter-of-fact tone.

"What? When? Where?"

"He collapsed and died on the subway at the Christie Street Station at 12:15. He is now at the Toronto Western Hospital, and you will have to go there and identify his body."

I explained that that was a little complicated, since I was blind.

There was a brief silence at the other end of the line. "I will contact my mother, and she will identify him." "Where is she?" he asked. "I went to the house to check that no one else was in trouble, and all I found was a cat who eyed me suspiciously and ran up to the attic."

"My mother is at her senior's club playing cards, but she will be home soon, and I will let her know."

The officer asked where I was and instructed me to wait for him to pick me up to take me to my father.

Hillcrest was not a big place, and there was no hope of secrecy. Many people, staff and patients, were excitedly chatting at the windows as the police car pulled up in front and the officer entered the building. Everyone was shocked when they realized it was me who was being driven away, but they knew better than to start nefarious rumours, although I took a lot of good-natured ribbing later.

I reached Peach and then called Pastor David, who drove Peach to the hospital. As I heard her footsteps in the corridor, I left Dad's cubical to meet her.

"Oh Ruthy, there I was, having fun with my friends, and had no idea Lester needed me."

"No, Peach, don't beat yourself up over it. They say he died immediately. His heart just stopped."

Somehow, surprisingly to me, when she entered the cubical and saw him, she seemed to revert back to a Newfoundland woman who had loved and cared for him, a vulnerable, wounded soldier, for fifty years. "Oh yes, that's him! Oh dear, dear, dear, oh Lester, my boy, my son, my son!"

We sat there for hours, awaiting the coroner. Ruby was very restless. I could find no way to settle her. Finally, we received word that Dad's body was released from care, and we were free to go and make funeral arrangements. Just as we were gathering our things, Ruby hopped up, putting her front paws on the stretcher. She looked close into my father's face and then jumped down. With that, the restlessness stopped, and she became very calm. It was as though she needed to see for herself or simply say goodbye.

Although it had been eight months since Sophie's death, I still had no peace about it. However, as we drifted through the steps of organizing a funeral service and burial for Dad, it suddenly occurred to me to ask if I could bury her with him. I knew it was against the law to bury animals in a human cemetery, but perhaps, as she has been cremated, they might let me put her with him. I had to gather some courage to ask Peach her thoughts on it, but when I explained to her that I needed to find some peace, she agreed. Pastor David made the inquiries and was told that if there was an official crematorium's certificate, they would put her urn in his casket. I put the paper shopping bag and certificate in Pastor David's care and he, along with the funeral director, tucked Sophie in beside Dad's right leg.

If the day Dad died was like a perfect spring day, then the day he was buried would have been described by him as the perfect winter day. We had a wild blizzard with snow blowing in every direction at once. Consequently, many friends and family who lived out of town were unable to attend, as the roads were too treacherous. As we carefully stepped through the cemetery to the graveside, I had Peach clinging desperately to my right arm, trying not to fall, with Ruby on my left side leaping and jumping to try and catch as many snowflakes in her mouth as possible. She was no help whatsoever, but she was entertaining under the grim circumstances.

The First Nation Canadians say that when we die, the crows come to take our souls away. Interestingly, despite the blustery, snowy weather, there were crows circling Dad's grave; that is, until we started to pray, at which time, they flew away. As we left the graveside, I said "Goodbye, Dad" and "Goodbye, Sophie," and for the first time in months, I felt peace.

Eight days later, we received a curious phone call from a neighbour of Peach's sister, Florence. She reported that Florence hadn't taken in her newspaper and was not responding to calls or knocks on her door. The building superintendent was notified and, upon entering the apartment, found that Aunt Florence had died in her sleep. Like Dad, it was completely unexpected. She had been at the funeral and appeared fine. We were still reeling from Dad, but life often does not take such things into consideration. It was especially hard on Peach, as she had been close to Florence her entire life: they shared books, movies, and the same sense of humour.

Although it is recommended that one not make any major changes for the first year after the death of a spouse, I asked Peach to consider moving into my house with me.

She thanked me but said no. "Honey, we have a good mother-daughter friendship, and I would like to keep it that way. Two adult women should never live under the same roof together. It only causes conflict and results in heartache."

I didn't want to ask her how lesbians managed, but I am sure she would have had an answer.

"Ruth, I will stay here until the Lord tells me it is time to leave. Now, I will admit that He may tell me through you and, if that is what happens, so be it."

CHAPTER 21

Gradually, Peach and I developed a new routine. I often dropped in to see her after work, and she came to visit me on Saturdays. Marilyn would join us, and we would play three-handed euchre and have breakfast or lunch together. Peach loved it. In the meantime, I had a decision to make: What would I do about the application and letter of intent sitting on my desk? Initially, I thought the best thing would be to put studying aside for a future date, but then it occurred to me that not embarking upon the degree would not change anything. I spoke with Peach about it and, in her usual positive fashion, she encouraged me to apply and put the rest in the Lord's hands.

I was delighted to receive my acceptance. The course was scheduled to start in September, where I would be part of an online class with students from several countries. Due to the different time zones, lecturer questions and student contributions would be asynchronous. That is, the students in the UK or Africa might contribute in the evening, and the Canadians would read their comments and make our contributions when we got home from work. I was in touch with the course leads, Gillian Jordan and Lynne Jump, who were very encouraging and supportive, and it was all sounding better and better. However, it is here that I must admit that I occasionally possess an overabundance of enthusiasm fuelled by trust or perhaps naiveté as I plunge headlong into things without fully investigating the logistics of my participation.

It never occurred to me that the online program might not be accessible with my screen-reading technology. I use a screen reader called JAWS for Windows, which I manipulate to read the computer screen. I type, and the computer talks. I don't talk to the computer—well, not with any polite words, anyway.

The University of Greenwich's online master's degree was using a fairly new program called Web Course Tools, or WebCT. However, the Lord has never put me in a situation without putting others there to help. The course had an IT support person, Shirley Ambrose, who was eager to work with me to ensure that technology would not stand in the way of my success.

Within WebCT, there was a general area where lecturers and students posted their questions and comments, and discussion threads evolved. However, there was also a student chat room, closed to staff, for the purpose of non-course-related socializing. Unfortunately, that part of the program was also inaccessible to me. My very kind and supportive classmates decided that if I could not access the student chat room, then no one else would go there either. Today, with improvements in screen-reader technology and program accessibility, the course might offer much more flexibility. However, in 2002, it allowed me just enough to participate in the course requirements.

The other difficult issue unique to my situation was the reading material that was not on the computer or in Braille. I had books and reams of articles that had to be read and researched. Fortunately, I had a scanner that, in essence, took pictures of the pages and converted the pages into text that the computer would then read back to me. The books generally contained a clear, simple font that the scanner easily identified and read well. However, that was not always the case with articles sent to me by other people or provided by the library.

Unfortunately, reproduced copies are often unclear. In such a situation, the results can be completely unintelligible. For instance, the scanner might interpret "I love you" as, "I l@ve y@u." I would have to listen to it, try and figure out what it was supposed to be saying, and when I did, I would go back and change all the @'s to o's and then reread the article. Often, there would be three or four letters consistently changed to something else and, if it involved a string of incorrect letters or symbols in a row, it would almost drive me mad. However, I painstakingly corrected each letter in the computer and, after rereading the article, would determine whether the article was relevant or not for my purpose. When one considers that this issue might arise for four or five pages of forty or fifty articles, one can imagine the time and frustration. One of my high school teachers once described me as tenacious, and I wasn't much pleased, but I can't think of another characteristic I'd need if I want to succeed.

I would not be exaggerating to say that working full-time while working on a very demanding master's of science degree with added practical complications was challenging. Furthermore, I also had to look after myself and Ruby, and I could not neglect Peach. I studied four evenings per week, giving myself one night for laundry, shopping, and so on. I studied Saturday mornings and kept Saturday afternoons open for a visit with Peach. As always, I kept the Sabbath holy with church and rest. It was a very structured life, but it needed to be so. Happily, I successfully completed all the coursework, followed by a year of research, data analysis, and the writing of my thesis. I submitted my dissertation in September 2005, exactly three years from the beginning of the course. At the same time, the Toronto Film Festival was on, and our dear friend, Claire Jennings, was in town for the premier of her film *Wallace & Gromit: The Curse of the Were-Rabbit*.

Claire came to my home for lunch with Peach and me, and we had a lovely afternoon until Claire asked Peach if she would be coming to England for my graduation.

"No, Ducky," she replied. "I don't think I could manage it."

"Blanche, if you don't come with her, it would be completely selfish!"

"Ooh, steady on," I interjected. There was no more said about it that day. I am not suggesting that Claire was wrong in what she said, but Peach adored her, and I didn't want anything to hurt that. Furthermore, I never expected Peach to fly to England with me. She was very proud of me. There was no doubt about that, but I knew that she would want to stay back in the shadows like she did whenever I received recognition for academic or other achievements. Although it would be impossible, she feared being an embarrassment to me due to her lack of formal education beyond grade nine—although she was more well-read and had better social graces than anyone I had ever met.

The next morning, Peach called me to say that Claire was right. "It would be selfish of me not to go to your graduation, and so I will when the time comes." I was surprised and thrilled and grateful to Claire for her courage to speak up.

Claire graciously sent us VIP tickets for the film in Toronto, which was a wonderful way to celebrate the end of my studies. Somewhat frail, Peach was given a chair to sit by the red carpet and everyone on the carpet, including Helena Bonham Carter, waved to her and said hello as they ran past into the hall. She felt like a celebrity herself. It was a great night.

The best Christmas gift that year was the letter from Greenwich stating that I had successfully completed the requirements for the master of science degree.

I can still hear Peach saying, "My daughter, my blind daughter has a master of science degree. Ruth, you can't take credit for the gifts that God has given you, but you can take credit for your will to do something with those gifts. That is what I am most proud of: your will to use your gifts."

Peach's increasingly frail health was diagnosed as kidney failure for which she underwent regular injections, intravenous medications, and procedures to change a stent in her ureter every six weeks. It was tough, but she never complained. She would only say, "I am blessed to have the life I have had, and one can't get old without something going wrong."

My graduation was scheduled for July 24, 2006. Fortunately, the UK animal quarantine laws had changed in the previous October, another blessing from God, allowing me to bring Ruby along. I was permitted two guests at the ceremony, so I invited Marilyn and Peach. It meant a lot of organizing, as all of Peach's procedures and treatments had to be timed accordingly, but all her specialists felt the trip would be the best medicine for her. I also wanted to visit my dear friends from physiotherapy school Dewi and Helen Perkins, who lived in North Wales, and we had an invitation to visit the IT specialist Shirley Ambrose at her home in the south near the New Forest. As I couldn't leave anything to chance, I organized the flight, hotel, trains—first class for Peach—and all the transportation and connections in between.

As we flew over England, heading for Heathrow, Marilyn and Peach were startled by the brown look of everything. They were used to the signature verdant pastures, but England was having one of the hottest, driest summers on record. On graduation day, it was thirty-six degrees—almost unheard of in London. I was already very warm in a two-piece dress with a silk camisole when I was taken in to be gowned and photographed.

As they blanketed me in a heavy wool robe and hood, I was asked whether Ruby would be accompanying me on the platform. "Yes," I replied, "I wouldn't be able to find the platform without her."

"Well, everyone on the platform must be gowned," they stated.

It is here that I must say, *only in Britain!* With that, two otherwise digni-fied adults struggled to put a master's hood on Ruby. Remember, Ruby was a very fluffy golden retriever, and it was a stifling hot day. She was having none of it. I could hear the kerfuffle as she danced about with a woman and man saying, "Now, stand still. That's a good girl."

I finally decided that I had better help them. "Just tell her she's pretty," I called over to them as a third person tried to balance a mortarboard on my head.

Desperate, they did as I suggested. "You're a pretty girl, such a very pretty girl." With that, Ruby came to attention. Standing absolutely still, she allowed them to drape her in a wool hood that started at her neck, extended to just above the tip of her tail, and hung down to her paws on both sides. All that was exposed was her head, toes, and the tip of her wagging tail. Hot or not, she was prepared to put up with it. Like women in stiletto heels, comfort be gone—anything to be pretty. Did I mention she was a diva? Her furry little mind was probably thinking, *I could use a little citronella behind my ears.*

The photo session included a shot with Peach and me together. She was so pleased. "Ruth, when I die, I don't want a whole lot of photos in the funeral parlour—just the one with the two of us on your graduation day. That one is my favourite."

As Ruby and I crossed the platform to receive my degree, I touched my cap to say thanks to Peach. "Thanks for sending me away to Brantford to learn to read. You may not have known what would become of me, but you never held me back from reaching for the stars."

Claire took Peach out for a posh afternoon tea at The Library while Marilyn and I went on the London Eye. Peach loved it and often spoke how being there with Claire made her feel like a grand lady. All in all, it was a wonderful trip, and when the two weeks were up, Peach didn't want to go home.

As we settled into our seats on the plane, she asked me if we could come back again.

"Yes, Peach, I would be delighted to bring you back for another adventure." Somehow, though, without saying it, we both knew that was not likely.

CHAPTER 22

In the spring of 2007, I developed some medical issues that I felt needed some attention. I had recently signed on with a new family physician. Tests revealed a large cyst on my left ovary. She informed me that she had made an appointment for me with a gynaecologist and that I should be prepared for more tests. As she held the door, ushering me out of her office, her final statement was, "Because we can't be sure that you don't have cancer." With that, the door was closed. I am not sure what I expected, but it wasn't that. Of course, I knew it could be cancer. However, a reassuring pat on the shoulder might have helped.

A few days later, I walked into the office of the gynaecologist where there were a few women, all happily pregnant, waiting to see the doctor. A woman asked me if it was my first visit and said that the doctor was very nice and gentle. The receptionist guided me into the examination room, and I was instructed to disrobe from the waist down and cover myself with a paper sheet. I sat nervously on the table while Ruby sat on the floor beside me. Suddenly, there was a knock on the door, and Ruby began to bark. A male voice asked if he could come in. The door opened slightly, and the doctor squeezed in, closed the door, and put his back against it.

"No dogs allowed," he said.

"She is my guide dog."

"No dogs allowed!" he repeated.

"She is my guide dog, sir."

"I can see that, but she is not allowed in my clinic."

"It is against the law to deny her access to this clinic, sir."

"This is my private clinic and, therefore, my laws."

"This is part of the public health-care system, sir, of which we are both a part, and you cannot deny me access with her."

He started to raise his voice. "Why couldn't you leave the dog at home?"

"How would I get here? She is my guide, and she is how I managed to find this place."

Still yelling: "Well, why does she have to be so big?"

Ruby wasn't big. She was only fifty-six pounds.

"I might not mind a Chihuahua," he snapped. It was a ridiculous statement, but that was the least of my issues. It quickly became a very toxic environment. I felt threatened and very vulnerable. I was being yelled at by a doctor who was standing with his back against a closed door with me sitting in front of him, half naked. Clearly, he was afraid of dogs, but at that moment, he was far more intimidating than she was. He suddenly got up his nerve, snatched up my file, and blurted, "I don't even know why you are here!"

"I believe I have a large cyst on my ovary," I offered.

"It's not that big, and I wouldn't do anything about it," he sniffed dismissively, and I was ordered to get dressed and go.

Fighting tears, I shook all the way home. I was shocked and angry about the treatment I had received. I called Marilyn to tell her what had happened, as she was eager to know what the doctor had to say. She, too, was shocked by his behaviour. I was not eager to tell Peach. Although I knew I could tell her anything, I wanted to protect her from what I had been through and the added stress to me. I decided immediately to call the College of Physicians and Surgeons of Ontario (CPSO) to report my experience. In complete contrast, I spoke with a woman there who was kind and supportive.

"He does not have the right to deny you access," she assured me knowingly, "and I will look into this issue and get back to you."

When I recounted the episode to some of my doctor colleagues at the hospital, they also were shocked and disappointed. My medical director, John Flannery, took me into his office and asked what he could do to help me. I didn't think there was anything at that time, but I would certainly let him know if anything came up later.

As I was about to leave, he said, "I am so sorry that this has happened to you, of all people, one of the most compassionate and best patient advocates I have ever met."

The CPSO suggested that I take whatever avenue was at my disposal to sue him for some financial settlement. "All doctors understand is money, and that is the best way to get through to them," I was told.

"No," I said, "I am not about punishment, but about remediation. He needs to know the law and his responsibility within it."

The receptionist had not been bothered about the dog, and I could have left Ruby behind the desk with her while I was examined if that made the doctor more comfortable, but that would have required a discussion, and that gynaecologist was not interested in civilized communication. My preference was for the CPSO to insist that he undertake some education on guide dogs and the laws around accessibility.

Two incident investigators from the CPSO met with the doctor, who admitted he was afraid of dogs and that he had allowed himself to lose his temper and did, in fact, raise his voice. Their meeting took an hour, after which I was sent a letter of alibied apology. Although many people wanted me to call the newspapers and embarrass him, I accepted the letter and left it at that. If two investigators from the CPSO meeting with him for an hour did not prick his conscience, then nothing would. Anything more from me would be vindictive, and vindictiveness is never classy.

Meanwhile, I still had a cyst on my left ovary that was increasing in size and needed attention, no matter what that doctor had said. I returned to my family physician, who made another appointment with another gynaecologist who was kind and certainly could be described as warm and fuzzy.

My appointment with the new surgeon was near the end of June. She palpated the now very large cyst and said, "Oh, its firm."

There was a brief but awkward silence in the room, as we both knew that firm was not a good sign. She excused herself and left. This time, Marilyn had accompanied me, and I was glad to have her there, especially as I awaited the doctor's return. Once back, she explained that she had gone to rearrange her surgical schedule, as she wanted to remove the cyst as soon as possible.

Before leaving, I added, "I would rather you didn't take my ovary." Like my father, I didn't care for the idea of bits of my body being excised.

The doctor reassured me that they rarely took ovaries in these situations.

At about the same time that June, Peach casually mentioned that she was having a great deal of difficulty climbing the stairs in her two-storey house. My brothers had talked about putting a bathroom on the main floor, but that was felt to be a little complicated with the size and age of the structure. Instead, I asked if she would like me to find her an apartment, and she said yes.

There was a lovely seniors' building around the corner from my house, and I thought that if Peach could get a unit in there, it would be perfect for both of us. I found the building management company and talked to the man at the top. He listed several buildings in the West End of Toronto that would all be suitable, but I explained my situation and that, preferably, I would like her in a building within walking distance in case she needed me in an emergency. We left it at that, and I explained to Peach that it could be months before she heard from them.

Meanwhile, my surgery day came, and I had other things to think about. Marilyn had offered to take me to the hospital, but I needed her to babysit Miss Ruby. I provided Marilyn with a bag of dehydrated liver and suggested for her to give Ruby a piece or two during the day to help with the separation anxiety. Ruby loved Marilyn, so I thought that would be the least disruptive arrangement.

As I left Marilyn's house, I could hear her saying, "No, you stay with me. That's a good girl." Once at the hospital, I called Marilyn just to check in, and I could hear Ruby whining in the background.

Marilyn sounded a little frantic. "I can't get her away from the door. She just keeps looking out and crying." I had to feel sorry for Marilyn, as I had only been gone twenty minutes, and there were hours of separation ahead.

My brother Ralph and his family were now living in Gananoque, in Eastern Ontario. When he heard about my surgery, he and his daughter, Emily, jumped in the car and drove the three and a half hours to Toronto to be at my side with Peach when I awoke. Although I had suggested to

Peach that she need not come to the hospital, as it would be a long and tiring day for her, I was relieved and comforted to wake and find her sitting by my bedside, holding my hand. Even though she was elderly and frail, there was no mistaking those big, soft, strong hands that had always meant reassurance and comfort like nothing else in all the world.

The doctor had spoken to Peach and my brother while I was asleep, but Peach had suggested to her that any information about me had to be delivered to me by her and only her. So when I awoke and asked Peach if she had seen the doctor, she only said that the doctor would be along, and she would speak to me. I was too groggy to worry about anything at that point. However, a few minutes later, the doctor was at my side.

"Ruth, we have some good news. We do not believe that there is any cancer. However, the cyst disintegrated when we went in. It had become a thin, white film that fell apart once we touched it. Unfortunately, it destroyed your ovary, and so I had no option but to remove the little stem of it that was left."

I understood it could not be helped, and I was not going to say anything more about it. I was just relieved and thankful that it wasn't any more sinister than that.

I was taken back to Marilyn's to recuperate, where Miss Ruby was standing inside the door going nuts. I stepped behind the door to protect myself from her possibly jumping on me. However, as the door slowly opened, she came out and immediately realized something was not right. She put on the brakes and became very calm. I sat on the sofa, and she gently stepped up and sat down beside me and was nothing but sweet and attentive. However, Marilyn was worn out, the bag of dried liver was almost completely empty, and I'm quite sure Marilyn didn't eat any of it.

The next day, Peach received a call from the gentleman at the building management company saying that a unit was available in the building around the corner from my house. She looked at it that day and decided to take it. It was perfect for her—a two-bedroom unit at the top of a five-storey building with views of people's gardens and the activity coming and going from the town hall next door. We were surprised at how quickly the apartment had become available, but it was another example of God's faithfulness. She was all settled in within a month. She was asked many times how she could just leave a house she had lived in for fifty-one years.

"Easily," she would say. "I just closed and locked the door behind me and kept going forward."

"But Blanche, your children were born there, and your memories are there."

"No, Ducky, my memories are with me, and I have so little life ahead of me that I can't afford to waste any of it by dwelling on the past."

Initially, Peach was able to walk the short distance to my house with her walker, but it was a bit of an incline, and she soon found it too tiring. However, that didn't matter. Ruby and I could get to her in two to three minutes and did so frequently. There was a seniors' bus that took her shopping and to other outings, and she quickly made friends in the building and started attending painting classes that were offered weekly at the town hall. All in all, it was a blessing to both of us.

CHAPTER 23

Marilyn and I were very involved with our church work, including teaching English to refugees. Gradually, we added travel to our list of activities, specifically cruising. I tended to get mentally tired with working full-time, my church responsibilities, and caring for Peach and our lovely refugees. Marilyn had done a great deal of travel over the years, and we both enjoyed it, so we decided to take some adventures together. It was only by getting completely away from the telephone and email that I could relax. I didn't like leaving Peach, although my brothers were always very supportive and did a lot to help her with shopping and fixing things around the apartment. Friends from church would phone her, and my dear friends Carol and Dorothy would visit her and bring food. I think she was glad to see me go for a while so she could get the others' attention. Did I mention she was a diva? Perhaps that is why she and Ruby were so well connected.

Oh yes, Ruby. She was enjoying her life with me—going to work every day and cruising around the world and all the attention that came with it. However, in April of 2010, she turned ten years old, was starting to have difficulty seeing in the dark, and was getting stressed more easily. She became terrified of thunderstorms. There was nothing specifically wrong, just age. In conversation with the Guide Dog Foundation, I was advised to consider retiring her. My heart sank! How could I retire a dog who couldn't stand one minute away from me? I knew that other guide dog handlers had kept some of their dogs when they retired them, and I thought that that might be what I would have to do with Ruby. She would have to stay home when I went to work with a new dog, but I thought she might accept it if I hired a dog walker to come and take her out for a couple of hours each day. Peach loved the idea, as she couldn't bear the thought of Ruby leaving us. If I told Ruby we were going to see Nanny, our term for grandmother, Ruby would go nuts, and as soon as she saw her, she would throw herself across Peach's lap, wrap her front paws around her neck, and squeal while kissing her face and ears.

Over the years, many people had asked if I would consider them for adoption if I retired Ruby. However, when the time came, there were no takers. Ruby was such a physically and willfully strong dog that no one felt they could handle her. Furthermore, everyone was aware of her separation anxiety, and no one was prepared to work through it. I had hoped that someone would, at least, step forward and volunteer to look after her for the two weeks while I was away at the Foundation getting my new dog, but no one was even willing to do that. I felt terrible for Ruby, whom I adored, and a little let down myself. Consequently, I had no choice but to find someone who would adopt her from outside our circle.

Barb at the Foundation offered to help with the process. She suggested that I could bring Ruby back, and they would find someone eventually, but I was in no way going to just drop her off and hope for the best. She was too valuable and precious to me, and I felt that would be dishonouring her faithful service.

At the eleventh hour, Barb called me to say that she might have a family to adopt her. Barb and I had a friend at the Foundation, Phyllis, who had died of cancer; while she was going through her treatments, she was given great support and kindness by a couple from her church, Tom and Pat. Consequently, I was familiar with their names, although I had never met them. Apparently, Pat's father, an elderly retired New York City police officer, had come to live with them, as he was failing to thrive at home on his own. However, his emotional state had not improved much with the move. They asked what they could do to help him.

He replied, "I just want a dog to pet for the rest of my life."

Days before I was to travel to the Foundation, Tom had mentioned his father-in-law's predicament to Barb. Bells went off in Barb's head: Ruby!

Knowing how kind this family had been to Phyllis, it was a pleasure and relief to consider them as a possible loving home for my sweet princess. On November 1, 2010, I took Ruby to her new home—a generous family living on an acre of property with a stream running by. Needless to say, she paced and cried for three days, but then it dawned on her: no work, lots of love, and lots of attention! She finally accepted it.

Immediately after dropping off Ruby and returning to the Foundation, I was presented with my new guide. We both cried all night—me for Ruby, and he for his familiar kennel. Either that, or he just didn't like me.

Ajay was a black lab/golden retriever cross, which made him a combination of Sophie and Ruby. However, he was male. They say that there is no difference in that both males and females make good guides, but there is a gender difference from a personality perspective that I do not believe can be denied. Yes, Sophie was a lady, and Ruby was a diva, but the one thing they had in common was that they always knew what they wanted and quickly decided what I needed. My boy, on the other hand, would do anything I asked him, but I had to ask because he just didn't *know*. Mind you, when we went to baseball games, he watched the play on the field. It was as though my females could read people and situations, and my male could read sports scores. Nevertheless, he was a big, gentle, cooperative, willing sweetheart—the perfect doggy husband, as it were.

In complete contrast to Ruby, Ajay didn't bark. I was told that when the dogs were being trained to be guides, two trainers took several out in the truck at the same time. When they opened the doors at the training destination, all the dogs eagerly wanted to be taken first. However, only the ones that were sitting quietly got that privilege. Apparently, Ajay was consistently taken first because of his obedient, quiet behaviour. However, Ajay's kennel mate, Brooklyn, a barking female golden retriever, was never taken ahead of the rest. On one occasion, Brooklyn managed to get Ajay in trouble by getting him to join her in the barking. The staff were surprised by his new bad behaviour and, to teach him a lesson, they took him last. He was not pleased. The next day, as they opened the van doors, Brooklyn was once again barking her head off, and when Ajay saw the staff, he smacked her in the head as if to say, Shut up, bitch, you got me in trouble yesterday! Gentle, yes. Stupid, no.

In late August of 2011, Marilyn, Ajay, and I took a cruise around England, Ireland, Scotland, and Wales. It was a wonderful trip. We especially enjoyed Scotland, where we went right up north to Kirkwall in the Orkney Islands. To get into Kirkwall, we had to take a shuttle bus. While there, we visited the splendid St Magnus Cathedral, rested in a friendly teashop, and did some shopping for Scottish woolens. Once back at the ship, we realized that our sweaters were much too big. I suggested that we go back and exchange them, but Marilyn wasn't feeling well and suggested we find someone at home for whom they would be the right size. That was not a solution for me. I gave Marilyn some Tylenol and suggested she go to bed while I went back into town. She protested that she would be too worried about me. "That's why I have Ajay," I said as I picked up the package and headed for the door.

Ajay and I joined the queue to get off the ship, found the bus, and headed back along the winding streets of Kirkwall. As we had stopped at several different places previously, I had to ask someone for directions to the specific shop. The ladies there remembered us and exchanged our beautiful sweaters for the correct sizes. Upon leaving the shop, I instructed Ajay to find the way back to the ship. With great confidence, he took me through the town to the bus, from the bus to the ship, and back to our cabin. Although I have had guide dogs since 1999, I never stop marvelling at their ability, and this was certainly an amazing feat, especially as we had only been together for ten months, and in that town only once. I felt triumphant.

As 2011 approached, Peach mentioned how she used to love the New Year's Eve parties I would hold at my house, where we would play cards and have dinner. Her mobility was becoming increasingly challenged, and even the four steps into my house were more than she could manage. I suggested she invite some of her friends from the building to her apartment for a little party.

"I don't know that they would want to come, and I don't have a nice tablecloth for my dining table, and I wouldn't like to serve even tea without one."

"Peach, to quote a wise woman, for every solution, there's a problem. You call your friends and leave the rest to me."

She was delighted to inform me that there would be four ladies gathering in her unit at seven o'clock on New Year's Eve. I arrived with a rose-coloured cloth for her table to match the pattern in her carpet. I also stocked her shelves with cheese, pâté, crackers, nuts, chips, and chocolate cream puffs, as well as a bottle of sherry. She felt that all that food was not necessary, as the ladies were arriving after dinner and so would not likely be hungry, but I assured her that once they all got chatting and laughing, they would need something to nibble on. Well, let me tell you, one lady arrived with a shrimp ring, another with a tray of homemade cookies and squares, and the third with a bottle of wine. I called at midnight to wish her a happy New Year, and all I could hear were gales of laughter in the background. I went straight to bed after I hung up the phone, but Peach's guests didn't leave until one thirty in the morning. Yes, all the food and drink was gone.

For her birthday in February, I planned a surprise that comprised her two favourite things—playing cards and breakfast. I hired the party room in her building, invited twelve people, and arranged a chef to cater a full hot breakfast. Peach was surprised and pleased, but her rapidly declining health was evident. She didn't even have the same stamina she had at the beginning of January. Enjoying the breakfast and cards took effort, followed by a lengthy recovery period.

In March, Peach fell while trying to get out of bed. She didn't appear to be injured, but she was unwell, so we called an ambulance. She spent several hours in the emergency room going through a battery of tests.

At one point, she asked me, "Ruth, am I going to die here?"

"I hope not, Peach."

A CT scan revealed a large mass in her lower-right abdomen. Later, she was visited by a young female oncologist who examined her and started talking about biopsies and treatments.

"No, Ducky," Peach said. "I am not having any more biopsies or treatments."

"Why am I here, then?" the doctor asked.

"I don't know," Peach replied, "I didn't send for you. When you were examining my tummy, did I see a cross around your neck?"

"Yes," the doctor said.

"Does that mean you are a Christian?"

"Yes," she replied.

"Doctor, let me explain something. You are young and enthusiastic about helping people, and I appreciate that, but I am old, and I will die, and you must accept that. I, too, am a Christian. I know that I am saved by the blood of Jesus Christ, and I am not afraid to die, because I am confident that once I leave this earth, I will be with Him in paradise."

With that, the doctor patted her arm, thanked her, and left.

The next visit from a doctor was her nephrologist with whom she had a great relationship. "Blanche, we are going to send you home, but we have designated you palliative, and so you will be looked after by a palliative care team."

"What does that mean, palliative?"

"It means that we think you have six months or less to live."

"But what if I live longer?"

"Well, if you live seven months, what are they going to do to us?" she replied, laughing. They knew Peach's sense of humour and felt comfortable to be lighthearted at such a serious moment, and she appreciated it.

I took her home with the understanding that that was where she wanted to die, and I would do everything in my power to fulfill her wish.

Managing the care of a declining elderly parent can be a bit of a juggling act, as it requires a lot of organization. I was willing to prepare her breakfast and help with her morning care, but I had to go to work, and she didn't rise until nine. I always said she was an early-to-bed and an early-to-rise person: she went to bed early in the morning and got up early in the afternoon. I also offered to go over after work and give her a bath, but she wouldn't hear of it.

"No honey, you are not going to be a caregiver all day at the hospital and then be a caregiver all evening as well. I don't want my last days on earth to be so onerous on you that you become resentful or for your last memories of me to be unpleasant. Let's just enjoy what time we have left together."

I hired someone to be at her apartment each day at nine to get her breakfast and make her bed. Bazada, a sweet Jamaican woman, also came on Saturdays to tidy the place. On Sundays, a university student who was a cancer volunteer would keep Peach company while I was at church.

Every Saturday morning, Marilyn and I would take a McDonald's breakfast to her and play cards. She loved a bacon egg McMuffin and that, along with a double-double coffee, would fuel her sufficiently to beat us. She didn't always win, but she did so often enough that I would ask myself why I even bothered. She thoroughly enjoyed our Saturday mornings, and so did we.

I knew all Peach's favourite foods well and prepared them for her on a regular basis. She especially loved pork chops with roasted onions and sweet potato oven chips. (Peach was making sweet potato fries forty years before anyone else had ever heard of them, but I digress.) I often made her dinner at my house, popped the food hot from the oven into containers, and would walk with Ajay to her apartment before it could get cold. I called it meals on paws.

On one occasion, I prepared all her favourites, but when I put it on the plate and placed it in front of her, she barked, "I don't like that! Why are you giving me that?"

I was shocked. First of all, my mother had never snapped at me in my life. Second, it was all the foods she preferred. Fighting tears, I simply said I was sorry, as I had mistakenly thought that it was what she liked. She wasn't happy, but she begrudgingly ate it.

The next day, I called Dr. Sasal, her nephrologist, and reported on Peach's sudden and complete change in personality.

"I am sorry Ruth. The calcium must be building in her blood again. I will order an IV infusion and hope it helps."

The palliative care nurse arrived, the treatment was given, and not only did it help, but she reverted back to the mother I had growing up. She was still physically frail, but cognitively brilliant—sharp and witty.

On Saturday morning, November 26, Marilyn and I went to Peach's for our usual breakfast and game of euchre. We let ourselves in, and there she was, the queen in her beloved armchair, waiting for her breakfast and an eagerly anticipated game of cards. She was her usual cheerful self, but once she finished her sandwich, she didn't come to the table. When I urged her to join us so we could start the battle, she asked to be given a few minutes. It was not like her. Whether she admitted it or not, Peach being slow to get to a card game was a powerful indication of just how unwell she was. She did eventually struggle to her seat and started to shuffle the deck. Despite her obvious deterioration, there were the usual silly one-liners as well as her boisterous rendition of Mozart's "Exsultate, jubilate" when she scored a point or two. She only managed half the number of hands we would normally play and asked to stop at that point, as she was getting too tired. The game ended with Mum, 35, me, 34, and Marilyn, 22. We left her back in her armchair feeling exhausted but exhilarated at her victory.

Later in the weekend, Peach mentioned that she was feeling cold in bed. Her apartment was a little chilly, so she had a portable heater, but she felt the problem was not having adequate bedclothes. She had a comforter, but it wasn't all that substantial, which had never mattered in the past, as she was always warm. In fact, Dad used to call her the human radiator. Although I had all her Christmas gifts purchased, I thought I had better get one more. She wasn't getting dressed anymore, so I had given her a thick velour dressing gown early so she could start enjoying it right away.

On Monday on my way home from work, I stopped in at a local linens and bedding shop. After much discussion with the proprietor, I settled on an ultra light microfiber duvet and a brightly coloured cover with a flowered pattern. I had also previously purchased a set of cotton flannel sheets and decided that Christmas was coming that night.

When I arrived at her apartment, she was in the living room, watching her beloved Coronation Street. I instructed her to stay there, as I had something to do in the bedroom and would call her when things were ready. Well, when it came to Christmas, Peach was like a little child. She could never wait to open things and was very curious about what Santa might bring. Not having children of my own, she was the one who always made Christmas enjoyable for me with her childlike excitement and love of the season. I heard her struggling down the corridor toward me, but I told her she would have to wait.

"You are not allowed to see Santa's elves at work."

"Put the light on," she said eagerly.

"You know that I don't need to put a light on."

"No, I know, but I have never quite understood how you manage so well in the dark."

"Well, that is part of the magic," I said, struggling to get a queen-sized duvet into its cover. "Santa's elves have to be able to work in the dark."

Once the bed was complete, I flipped the light switch, and Peach maneuvered her walker into the room.

"Oh Ruthy," she gasped, "does that ever look inviting. I think I will go to bed right now, if you will help me get ready."

I left her snuggled between the soft flannel sheets and completely enveloped by the big, puffy duvet with her cat, Isabel, purring beside her. If she wasn't warm enough in all that, I would have to tuck her into the oven. Later, she called me to say that her bed was just perfect and that she was nice and warm.

Over the next several days, Peach continued to sound like her old self, her voice strong and her thoughts clear. One night that week, she wanted me to know that if she could have any daughter in the whole world, she would still choose me. I, of course, reminded her that I felt the same way about her as my mother, but I had told her that many times over the years. The only difference was that this time, she didn't make any sarcastic retort.

On Friday, December 2, I called her from work as I did each morning. However, this morning was different. She didn't sound well, and she said so. I suggested that I come over immediately after work. She was enthusiastic about the idea and asked if I could bring her some soup. I did so, and she enjoyed a bowl of chicken vegetable, a particular favourite of hers.

We spent the entire evening together, her in her armchair and me in the rocker, just chatting and thoroughly enjoying each other's company. Of course, I had to sit quietly while Coronation Street was on, but I didn't mind, as there was pleasure to be derived out of her involvement with the story lines and characters. After the television program was over, she asked me what I would do if she died that night. I jokingly suggested that I would arrange a funeral. That led to a wonderful discussion about her favourite hymns—"The King of Love my Shepherd Is," "Breathe on Me Breath of God," "Thou Didst Leave Thy Throne," and "O Master, Let Me Walk with Thee"—and why they were so special. We also opened the Bible together and read her favourite passage, Psalm 139. She was comforted in the truth that there was nowhere we could go that God could not see us or where He was not with us. Wistfully, she stated that she only hoped that, during her lifetime, she had done something to express to God just how much she loved Him. I said that I hoped it was me. She also talked about Ruby and said how sorry she was that I had given her away. In fact, it was the one regret of her life. She thought that keeping her and arranging a dog walker was the perfect solution, and it would mean that she would still be able to visit with her. It broke my heart to hear her admit her feelings about it, but I understood, as I, too, was sorry that I'd had to give her away.

Then she gave me a piece of advice: "Don't let anything come between you and Marilyn."

"Peach, it takes two to tango."

"I know, Ruthy, but she is not a fool, and she won't let you go, because she has a good thing in you, and she knows it."

"Well, Peach, you know that I have loved her since we first met, and I have never been able to overlook my heart where she is concerned."

Finally, she suggested that I should go home, as I had to work in the morning. She didn't want me to help her get ready for bed, but rather assured me that she could manage it on her own. So I bid her goodnight, and Ajay and I left. I had just pulled my covers up when I thought I should call and make sure she was safely in her bed too. When she answered the phone, I knew that she was not.

"I need you," she said. "I am so sick and vomiting."

I assured her I was on my way and jumped into a sweatsuit, harnessed my sleeping dog, and we ran to her. I let myself in and found her in a mess and desperate. I cleaned her up and tucked her into bed. I offered to stay the night in the other room, but she insisted that she was now fine and that I should go home to get some sleep in the comfort of my own bed. Reluctantly, I left her.

One of my colleagues offered to work my Saturday shift, but I declined her kindness, as working on Saturday would mean having Monday off, and I sensed that my mother might need me even more come Monday. Bazada was there on Saturday morning, and I spent the evening with Peach, but, again, she insisted that I go home to sleep. I did so but set my clock to awaken early and go back to her first thing.

I was in the bathtub at six in the morning when the phone rang. It was Mum. Her breathing was laboured as she struggled to say, "Ruth, I need you."

Slightly panicked, I assured her that I was on my way and would be there in a matter of minutes. I think she felt that was too long, but there was no alternative. Once Ajay and I arrived, we found her in bed, gasping for breath and complaining of unbearable abdominal pain. Admitting that to me was alarming, as she had an extraordinarily high pain threshold. She's the woman who had five natural childbirths and said it wasn't all that bad—"I had toothaches worse." So all I could think was, *how bad was her pain?* I managed to find her medication and give her a dose. She asked whether I thought she should go to the hospital. I assured her that I would take her there immediately if that was what she wanted, but if she still preferred to remain at home, I would do my best to look after her. She said that she would prefer to be in her own bed, and I was relieved, as it was easier for me to attend to her in these familiar surroundings.

At seven thirty, the outside door buzzer rang. I was a little startled, as I could not imagine who would be there at that time on a Sunday morning. When I answered it, I was delighted to hear my brother Ralph's voice with his familiar, "Hey kid, let me in." He had awakened early and, knowing Peach was not doing well, felt it best to drive the three-plus hours to Toronto to see her and give me some support.

Together, we cared for her. I contacted the palliative care team and let them know of her decline and severe pain. They prescribed some hydromorphone, but no one came to see her that day. However, as the day went along, Paul dropped in and brought some needed supplies. John, his wife Heather, their children Kyle and Mara, and Mara's fiancé, Mike, also came for a visit. While they were all there, I took the opportunity to get out with Marilyn for a bite to eat and left the boys to have their own quiet time with her. During the afternoon, Christopher called and suggested that he would come over the next day to see her, but she discouraged him from that plan, as she felt she might not be there tomorrow. Christopher was startled by her apparent weakness and admission of her impending demise. He immediately got into his truck and made the hour drive down to the city.

That evening, as Ralph, Paul, Christopher, and I sat reminiscing in the living room, Peach started having some hallucinations in her bedroom. She called to me with some alarm, as she was very concerned that Ralph was feeding chocolate to my dog. I reassured her that everything was fine, but she protested that she saw him do it on television. Once we settled her again, we teased Ralph about getting in trouble with Mommy, and it helped to lighten the heavy atmosphere. However, she soon started imagining things again and called to Paul. Although she was unable to do anything for herself, including roll over in bed, she managed to sit up on the side of the bed and, reaching for her handbag, explained to Paul that she wanted a quarter so she could show him a magic trick. Fortunately, the hallucinations subsided, and she became quiet and restful. Some laypeople might think her sudden burst of energy and independence a hopeful sign of some improvement, but after years in health care, I knew it to be nothing more than potential disaster.

Recognizing that we could not leave her alone through the night, we each volunteered to stay. Christopher, not having to work in the morning, suggested that he could give the rest of us a break. Paul and I were grateful for the offer, but Ralph was adamant that he stay, as he was already lifting her from her bed and toilet, and she trusted him to look after her. However, he would then need to leave in the morning, as he had a noon meeting.

Monday morning came quickly. I rose very early and went up to Bloor Street to pick up a coffee and food for Ralph, as he needed to be on the road by seven thirty. He was grateful for the nourishment and took it as he reluctantly kissed Peach goodbye and went back to Gananoque. Paul arrived soon after but left again in search of some supplies that Peach needed now that she was bedridden.

Faithful as always, our beloved Bazada arrived to prepare Peach's breakfast. I met her at the door and explained that Peach would not be needing breakfast, but I would appreciate some help to wash and change her.

Bazada stayed with Paul and me all morning but left when Peach's doctor arrived. The doctor was very surprised to see how quickly Peach had deteriorated in such a few short days. I let Peach know that her friend Dr. Skalenda was there, and he addressed and kissed her with the tenderness of a man called to palliative medicine. Her blood pressure was almost imperceptible, and he informed Paul and me that it would be only a few hours or, at the very outside, two to three days. He sat and chatted with us for some time. It was nice just to have the company. He stated that whenever he visited Peach, it was unlike any of his other patients. He admitted that her positive attitude and deep faith did more for him than he ever did for her.

It was a very raw December 5, and Mom's apartment was chilly. As I sat by her bed, after the doctor left, she was restless and moaning softly. I inquired whether there was anything I could do for her.

In a raspy whisper, she gasped, "I am dying."

I reached out and touched her arm as I reassured her that it was okay. I reminded her that she was a wonderful mother and faithful servant of Jesus. I suggested that it was no longer necessary to struggle on, and she should feel free to let herself go into her Saviour's embrace. She became very quiet, and the room filled with calm. She said nothing else for some time, although, according to the others, she often opened her eyes and looked at us and around the room.

At one point, I said, "Hey, wait a minute. The last time we played cards, you won. If you leave me now, you will be forever the winner and me the loser."

Much to my surprise, she gave a weak laugh and whispered, "Yeah, pretty good, eh?"

To keep her comfortable, I turned her from side to side every hour or so. Later in the afternoon, as I tucked her new duvet around her back and shoulders while keeping her arms outside the covers, as I knew that was how she preferred to sleep, she whispered loudly, "Thank you."

I was humbled by her gratitude and assured her that it was not necessary. There was no place I would rather be or no one I would rather be with. My love and compassion for her at that moment were overwhelming. I kissed her soft cheek as I reminded her that I had always adored her. It was a moment in my relationship with my mother like no other.

The artist Esther Zeitlin once produced a piece depicting a fetus giving birth to its mother. Perhaps in that tender moment as we faced her death together, we had evolved into that inverse mother-daughter relationship that happens so often to so many but is really indescribable. Like birth, death is an intimate connection at the level of one's soul. Was I at that juncture, giving birth to her through death into life eternal?

As Christmas was three weeks away, I sang some of our favourite carols: "O Little Town of Bethlehem" and "Thou Didst Leave thy Throne," and then I felt compelled to sing the Good Friday hymn, "O Sacred Head, Now Wounded." The fourth verse says, "Be near me when I'm dying." Once I sang those words, Peach said in a clear, strong voice, "Amen!" and fell silent.

Ajay suddenly came bounding into the room for the first time all day. He nuzzled Peach's ear, as if to wake her up, until she reached out a hand to touch him. I told her it was my dog. I don't know whether she realized it was Ajay or thought it was Ruby, but it didn't matter. He then left as quickly as he came.

Paul joined me at her bedside, and the two of us talked and laughed as though it were just another evening. Mom's breathing became very shallow. I reminded Paul that the doctor had said she might stop breathing for up to thirty seconds before taking another breath. I had always heard about agonal breathing in my annual CPR certification. Of course, the agony is for the one who is struggling to breathe, but they are not alone. Paul thought that she was gone, but I knew it was not over yet, as I could feel the burning in my own chest as I willed her to breathe. We held her as she took one more gasp and was then at peace.

Paul whispered, "This is the way it was meant to be, wasn't it, Ruth? I am glad we were together with her."

I agreed, as I felt that we had just loved her into eternity.

(Almost) the end.

EPILOGUE

Although my passion for physiotherapy and the care of patients has never waned, I kept my promise to Peach and, on April 30, 2015, left the hospital for the last time. Marilyn and I began my retirement with a trip to Europe, and we continue to travel together, although she is elderly now. I was patient, never overlooked my heart, and know that we are soulmates. I am currently with my fourth guide dog, Darwin, and Ajay has retired, exchanging battling rush-hour traffic on the Toronto subway for couch-surfing with Marilyn. My brother Paul has always said that all I am is because of Peach, and I believe my story reveals this truth. Peach always said that the pain of death softens and that I would miss her, but I don't think she or I ever realized just how much.

All my brothers have married. John is a wonderful vegetarian chef and runs a B & B in Kingston, Ontario where he lives with his wife Heather. They moved within blocks of their children and grandchildren.

Christopher and his wife, Carol, live in Bradford, Ontario. He has retired from making soap for Lever Brothers, and they are simply enjoying their children and grandchildren.

Paul lives in Campbellford, Ontario, where he sells real estate and is learning to pilot an ultralight aircraft. His grandchildren don't live close, but he sees them frequently.

Ralph is in management in an animal-feed company and lives with his wife Sarah in northern Alberta. They moved there to be close to their daughter and grandchildren.

I am the only one living in Toronto now, but I hear from two or three of my brothers every week. They are more than brothers to me—they are dear friends!

What lies ahead? Only God knows, but in that, be assured that His plans are perfect!

Please visit:
http://www.ruthvallis.com/

ABOUT THE AUTHOR

Ruth Vallis lives in Toronto with her guide dog, Darwin. This is her first book, written after a thirty-two-year career in physiotherapy, mainly at the Toronto Rehabilitation Institute, where she entertained her patients with humorous or touching anecdotes to distract them from their pain or discomfort. Further to this end, she would not allow "organ recitals." That is what she called patients trying to one-up each other with lists of their kidney, liver, or heart ailments.

This book is dedicated to the memory of her mother, Blanche "Peach" Vallis, 1923–2011. Gone, but never forgotten!!!

Printed in Canada